Office for National Statistics

Economic & Labour Market Review

D1810145

Contents

Vol 2 No 11
November 2008 edition

Office for National Statistics

palgrave
macmillan

ISBN 978-0-230-21738-6
ISSN 1751–8326 (print)
ISSN 1751–8334 (online)

A National Statistics publication

National Statistics are produced to high professional standards set out in the National Statistics Code of Practice. They are produced free from political influence.

Not all the statistics contained within this publication are national statistics because it is a compilation from various sources.

The inclusion of reports on studies by non-governmental bodies does not imply endorsement by the Office for National Statistics or any other government department of the views or opinions expressed, nor of the methodology used.

About us

The Office for National Statistics

The Office for National Statistics (ONS) is the executive office of the UK Statistics Authority, a non-ministerial department which reports directly to Parliament. ONS is the UK government's single largest statistical producer. It compiles information about the UK's society and economy which provides evidence for policy and decision-making and in the allocation of resources.

The Director of ONS is also the National Statistician.

Palgrave Macmillan

This publication first published 2008 by Palgrave Macmillan, Houndmills, Basingstoke, Hampshire RG21 6XS and 175 Fifth Avenue, New York, NY 10010, USA

Companies and representatives throughout the world.

Palgrave Macmillan is the global academic imprint of the Palgrave Macmillan division of St. Martin's Press, LLC and of Palgrave Macmillan Ltd. Macmillan® is a registered trademark in the United States, United Kingdom and other countries. Palgrave is a registered trademark in the European Union and other countries.

A catalogue record for this book is available from the British Library.

Contacts

This publication

For information about this publication, contact the Editor, David Harper, tel: 020 7014 2036, email: elmr@ons.gsi.gov.uk

Other customer and media enquiries

ONS Customer Contact Centre
Tel: 0845 601 3034
International: +44 (0)845 601 3034
Minicom: 01633 812399
Email: info@statistics.gsi.gov.uk
Fax: 01633 652747
Post: Room 1015, Government Buildings,
Cardiff Road, Newport, South Wales NP10 8XG

www.statistics.gov.uk

You can find a downloadable version of this publication at www.palgrave-journals.com/elmr

Subscriptions

Annual subscription £210, single issue £37.50
To subscribe, contact Palgrave Macmillan, tel: 01256 357893, www.palgrave.com/ons

Copyright and reproduction

© Crown copyright 2008

Published with the permission of the Office for Public Sector Information (OPSI)

You may re-use this publication (excluding logos) free of charge in any format for research, private study or internal circulation within an organisation providing it is used accurately and not in a misleading context. The material must be acknowledged as Crown copyright and you must give the title of the source publication. Where we have identified any third party copyright material you will need to obtain permission from the copyright holders concerned.

For re-use of this material you must apply for a Click-Use Public Sector Information (PSI) Licence from:

Office of Public Sector Information, Crown Copyright Licensing and Public Sector Information, St Clements House, 2–16 Colegate, Norwich NR3 1BQ, tel: 01603 621000, www.opsi.gov.uk/click-use/index.htm

Printing

This book is printed on paper suitable for recycling and made from fully managed and sustained forest sources. Logging, pulping and manufacturing processes are expected to conform to the environmental regulations of the country of origin.

Printed and bound in Great Britain by Latimer Trend & Company Ltd, Plymouth, Devon

Typeset by Curran Publishing Services, Norwich

In brief

Changes to Income Support for lone parents and expected impact on Jobseeker's Allowance claimant count

The rules for qualifying for Income Support are changing for lone parents. From November 2008, lone parents with a youngest child aged 12 or over may not qualify for Income Support solely on the grounds of being a lone parent (subject to certain exemptions and conditions). New and repeat claimants will be affected from November 2008, whereas lone parents with an existing Income Support claim will be affected gradually throughout the year following the rule change. This change will then be introduced for lone parents with a youngest child aged 10 or over from October 2009, and a youngest child aged 7 or over from October 2010. Those affected may decide to make a claim for another benefit and if able will be encouraged to look for paid work.

Although lone parents will not be transferred directly to other benefits from Income Support, it is anticipated that a number of them, while looking for paid work, will claim Jobseeker's Allowance. This is not a change to the rules for claiming Jobseeker's Allowance, but is expected to have an impact on the level of people in the claimant count.

It will not be possible to directly measure the impact on the claimant count. This is because some lone parents are already looking for work and claiming Jobseeker's Allowance. Therefore, it will be impossible to know which new lone parent claimants of Jobseeker's Allowance would have been in the claimant count regardless of the rule change. Instead, it is intended to monitor the total number of lone parents within the Jobseeker's Allowance claimant count. Work has been commissioned by DWP to produce a time series of numbers of lone parents in the claimant count, which will be made available on the Nomis website (details are given below). Due to the way in which lone parents can be identified, the count of the number of lone parents in any period is likely to be published one month after the claimant count for that period. It is anticipated that this series will become available from early 2009.

More information

www.nomisweb.co.uk

Contact

Bob Watson
☎ 01633 455070
✉ bob.watson@ons.gsi.gov.uk

ONS Review of the Labour Force Survey

The Office for National Statistics (ONS) is conducting a project to review the use and structure of the Labour Force Survey (LFS). Reviews of this nature are normal within ONS to ensure that the statistics produced are as robust as possible. The review is being conducted as part of the Labour Market Division analysis team work programme and initially it will identify users of the LFS and the extent to which existing questions meet their needs.

The LFS is the largest continuous household survey of approximately 53,000 households in the UK. Because of the numerous publications produced from the LFS, it is likely that ONS is unaware of all of the users. Therefore, in order to ensure that the LFS review consults a broad spectrum of users, ONS is inviting those users and stakeholders who wish to be involved in the consultation to contact Debra Leaker, by 1 December 2008, using the contact details below.

Contact

Debra Leaker
☎ 01633 455874
✉ debra.leaker@ons.gsi.gov.uk

Virtual Microdata Laboratory quarterly workshop – innovation: what can we learn from the data?

The Virtual Microdata Laboratory (VML) is a secure research environment designed to allow government and academic research to be conducted on Office for National Statistics (ONS) microdata. The VML is run by the Microdata Analysis and User Support (MAUS) team who organise a quarterly workshop series to:

- create links and foster communication between researchers (both government and academic)
- develop specific research topics, and
- raise awareness of the research potential of ONS microdata

The latest quarterly workshop, held on 10 October, took innovation as its central theme and explored a variety of topics.

Mark Pollard, from ONS, gave a detailed presentation about the innovation surveys which ONS conducts, and planned future developments. Mark also encouraged discussion about the difficulties of comparing 'identical' surveys across different European countries, for example, ensuring a consistent interpretation of the questions by respondents to the UK Innovation Survey. Mark Franklin and Peter Stam (ONS) also contributed to the discussion on European comparisons, by presenting their findings on the information and communication technology (ICT) impact assessment. This is a EuroStat-funded multicountry study linking microdata sources 'to identify how ICT adoption affects business behaviour and performance'. Their work provides some evidence that innovation boosts productivity, after controlling for ICT usage.

The academic papers presented provided much discussion about the conceptions behind innovation and investment. Highlights of the day included:

- Xiaolan Fu (Oxford) who presented work on how collaboration and regulation affect financial innovation
- Mario Kafouros (Leeds) who examined the relationship between international diversification, external scientific knowledge and performance
- Annarosa Pesole (Queen Mary) who outlined UK estimates of investment spending on design
- Richard Harris (Glasgow) who presented results on the factors influencing R&D at a regional level
- Ray Lambert and Marion Frenz (DIUS) who looked at firm performance and the associated types of innovation
- James Foreman-Peck (Cardiff) who caught policy makers' attention with his work on industrial and innovation policy.

Contact

Thea Thomas

☎ 01633 455844

✉ maus@ons.gsi.gov.uk

International information technology impacts

On 23 October, the Office for National Statistics (ONS) presented new work on information and communication technology (ICT) impacts in the business sector at the annual Productivity Conference organised by Statistics Sweden. Over the last two years, ONS has led a group of 13 EU statistics offices in a programme, funded by Eurostat, to develop new ways of using data linking, to get more useful information and indicators out of survey returns on ICT. The project also set out to test, using other countries' statistics, earlier UK conclusions showing strong productivity effects associated with high-speed internet use.

The results, which will be posted on Eurostat's website later in November, showed that:

- productivity effects of high-speed internet are pervasive across the EU, measured at industry level
- productivity effects measured at the level of individual businesses are much more variable, especially in the service industries
- the difference is largely due the effects of ICT in making markets more innovative and competitive, speeding up both price competition, and the spread of new products and services from successful firms, and
- the UK is among those countries where ICT use is most strongly associated with higher productivity

The project has been successful in developing technology use indicators which are consistent with national accounting and other economic and labour market data. This will enable analysts to look at technology impacts across countries in a consistent way, and show how trends and effects are different. It will also spur the development of ways to integrate data on technology use into economic analysis – so that changes in productivity can be better understood.

The Organisation for Economic Co-operation and Development and the European Commission are looking to take this further – beyond the area of ICT for which this study is a pilot.

Details of the Statistics Sweden Productivity Conference 2008 can be found at the address given below.

Contact

Tony Clayton

☎ 020 7014 2031

✉ tony.clayton@ons.gsi.gov.uk

Mark Franklin

☎ 01633 455981

✉ mark.franklin@ons.gsi.gov.uk

UPDATES

Updates to statistics on www.statistics.gov.uk

7 October
Index of production

Manufacturing: 1.1% three-monthly fall to August
www.statistics.gov.uk/cci/nugget.asp?id=198

9 October
UK trade

Deficit narrowed to £4.7 billion in August
www.statistics.gov.uk/cci/nugget.asp?id=199

10 October
International productivity

New estimates for 2007
www.statistics.gov.uk/cci/nugget.asp?id=160

13 October
Producer prices

Factory gate inflation falls to 8.5% in September
www.statistics.gov.uk/cci/nugget.asp?id=248

14 October
Inflation

September: CPI up to 5.2%; RPI up to 5.0%
www.statistics.gov.uk/cci/nugget.asp?id=19

15 October
Average earnings

Pay growth slows in the year to August
www.statistics.gov.uk/cci/nugget.asp?id=10

Unemployment

Unemployment rate rises to 5.7% in three months to August
www.statistics.gov.uk/cci/nugget.asp?id=12

20 October
Public sector

September: £5.9 billion current budget deficit
www.statistics.gov.uk/cci/nugget.asp?id=206

23 October
Corporate profitability

14.4% in Q2 2008
www.statistics.gov.uk/cci/nugget.asp?id=196

Retail sales

Underlying growth slows in September
www.statistics.gov.uk/cci/nugget.asp?id=256

24 October
GDP growth

Economic decreased by 0.5% in Q3 2008
www.statistics.gov.uk/cci/nugget.asp?id=192

Index of services

0.3% three-monthly fall into August
www.statistics.gov.uk/cci/nugget.asp?id=558

28 October
UK net worth

£7.0 trillion at end-2007, an increase of £506 billion on previous year
www.statistics.gov.uk/cci/nugget.asp?id=479

31 October
Local employment

Highest employment rate outside London, 89.6%, in Tewkesbury, Gloucestershire
www.statistics.gov.uk/cci/nugget.asp?id=252

Local unemployment

Highest unemployment rate outside London, 9.9%, in Leicester
www.statistics.gov.uk/cci/nugget.
asp?id=1606

Local inactivity

Lowest inactivity rate of 8.2% in Test Valley, Hampshire
www.statistics.gov.uk/cci/nugget.
asp?id=1013

FORTHCOMING RELEASES

Future statistical releases on www.statistics.gov.uk

5 November
Index of production – September 2008

6 November
New construction orders – September 2008

10 November
Producer prices – October 2008

11 November
MM22: Producer prices – October 2008

UK trade – September 2008

12 November
Labour market statistics – November 2008

MM19: Aerospace and electronics cost indices – August 2008

13 November
Digest of engineering turnover and orders – September 2008

Public and private breakdown of labour disputes

14 November
Monthly review of external trade statistics – September 2008

17 November
MM17: Price Index Numbers for Current Cost Accounting (PINCCA) – October 2008

18 November
Consumer price indices – October 2008

20 November
Public sector finances – October 2008

Retail sales – October 2008

SDM28: Retail sales – October 2008

21 November
ICT and e-commerce 2007, UK business

24 November
Focus on consumer prices – October 2008

25 November
Business investment provisional results – Q3 2008

Public sector finances: supplementary (quarterly) data

26 November
Index of services – September 2008

Market sector GVA

Services producer price index (experimental) – Q3 2008

UK output, income and expenditure – Q3 2008

Economic review

November 2008

Anis Chowdhury
Office for National Statistics

SUMMARY

GDP output contracted in 2008 quarter three - driven by negative growth in services, manufacturing and construction output. On the expenditure side, household spending and business investment showed a weak position in the second quarter. The current account deficit widened in quarter three, whilst the goods trade deficit narrowed slightly. The labour market showed further signs of weakening in 2008 quarter three; average earnings remain relatively subdued. Public sector finances deteriorated in September 2008. Consumer price inflation increased further in September 2008 and was considerably above the Government's inflation target. Producer output and input price inflationary pressures persisted in quarter three.

GROSS DOMESTIC PRODUCT

Growth contracts in third quarter

The preliminary estimate of GDP growth for the third quarter of 2008 is now available. GDP growth is estimated to shrunk compared with flat growth in the previous quarter. Growth fell by 0.5 per cent, a weakening from zero per cent growth in the previous quarter. The initial estimate for the annual rate of growth deteriorated sharply growing by a subdued 0.3 per cent, down from 1.6 per cent growth

in the previous quarter. It should be noted that these estimates are based on the output approach to measuring GDP. The headline figure will be firmed up later as more data becomes available (**Figure 1**).

This contraction in the UK economy was largely due to a decline in growth in service sector output. Industrial production growth continued to display weakness for the fifth successive quarter, with a deeper deceleration in output in quarter three compared to the previous quarter. The fragility in total production was broad based but was mainly driven by a sharp

contraction in manufacturing output growth. The output of the electricity, gas and water supply and mining and quarrying (including oil and gas) industries also recorded negative growth. The slowdown in GDP growth was also led by a faster contraction in the output of the construction sector compared with the previous quarter.

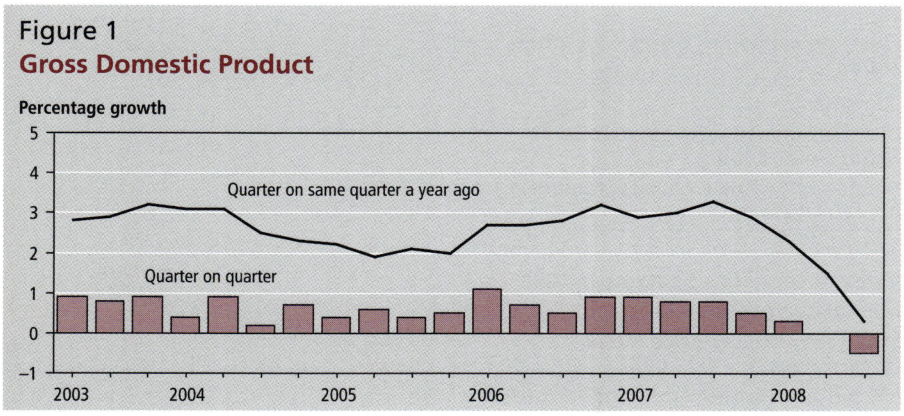

OTHER MAJOR ECONOMIES

Global growth showed mixed fortunes in quarter two

Data for 2008 quarter two for the other major OECD countries are now available. Performance appears to be somewhat mixed, although overall the picture is of weakening global growth compared with the previous quarter.

US GDP growth accelerated in 2008 quarter two achieving a rate of 0.8 per cent compared to 0.2 per cent in the previous quarter. The improvement in GDP growth was largely driven by increased consumer spending and which may partly be attributed to the government fiscal stimulus plan between late April and Early July. Net exports also contributed to growth for the fifth consecutive quarter helped by a weak dollar and imports contracting sharply. Government spending also boosted growth as well as non-residential investment. Residential investment on the other hand continued to contract – for the tenth consecutive quarter.

Japan's GDP weakened in the latest quarter. Growth contracted by 0.6 per cent in quarter two compared to an increase of 0.8 per cent in the previous quarter. Most components of GDP decreased. Lower growth was primarily led by contraction in private consumption. Residential investment also decreased in the latest quarter after having posted positive growth in the previous quarter. Business investment recorded virtually flat growth. Net exports also subtracted from growth in the second quarter – for the first time since 2004 quarter four.

Euro-zone growth deteriorated in the latest quarter. According to Eurostat's estimate, euro area GDP growth contracted by 0.2 per cent after increasing by 0.7 per

Figure 1
Gross Domestic Product

Percentage growth

cent in quarter one – the first contraction since the early 1990's. Growth for the three big mainland EU economies – Germany, France and Italy – also showed a weakening picture compared with the previous quarter.

German GDP contracted by 0.5 per cent in 2008 quarter two – for the first time in four years. This follows growth of 1.3 per cent in quarter one. All the components of demand with the exception of government expenditure contracted during the second quarter with the sharpest falls recorded for household consumption and construction investment.

French GDP growth contracted by 0.3 per cent in quarter two and the first decline since 2002 quarter four. Private consumption recorded virtually flat growth. Overall investment contracted markedly, led by a fall in household investment. Exports also subtracted from growth with exports registering the sharpest fall since 2001 quarter four.

Italian GDP fell by 0.3 per cent in the latest quarter following growth of 0.5 per cent in quarter one. The contraction was mainly driven by weakness in private consumption, investment and net exports.

FINANCIAL MARKETS

Share prices fall; pound depreciates

Equity performance has displayed volatility over the last couple of years. In 2008 quarter three, share prices fell back substantially into negative territory following positive growth in the previous quarter. In 2008 quarter three, the FTSE All-Share index decreased by around 10 per cent compared to a rise of around 2 per cent in quarter two. The fall was mainly driven by a sell-off in shares in the financial and banking sectors. The weakness in share prices may be attributed to global growth concerns particularly in terms of recessionary fears, brought on by continued financial sector liquidity problems and its

negative impact on the real economy.

In the currency markets, 2008 quarter three saw sterling's broad average value continuing to depreciate. The pound's value against the dollar fell by around 4 per cent compared to a depreciation of around 1 per cent in the previous quarter. In October 2008 the pound fell below the $1.60 mark for the first time in five years. Against the euro, sterling's value was virtually flat in the third quarter, following depreciation of around 5 per cent in the previous quarter. Overall, the quarterly effective exchange rate depreciated by approximately 2 per cent in 2008 quarter three after depreciating by approximately 3 per cent in the previous quarter (**Figure 2**).

The recent movements in the exchange rate might be linked to interest rate and growth factors. Exchange rate movements can be related to the perceptions of the relative strengths of the US, the euro and UK economy. The depreciation of the pound against the dollar in quarter three may have come in response to fears about lower growth and a possible recession in the UK economy, compared with the better outlook for the US and therefore the prospect of greater easing of interest rates in the UK to stimulate the economy. Indeed, the Bank of England reduced interest rates by 50 basis points in October 2008 which left UK rates standing at 4.5 per cent. This together with earlier cut in UK interest rates may have made the pound less appealing to investors compared to other currencies. Another factor for the relative strength of the dollar against the pound may have been due to the recent fall in oil prices with lower oil prices seen as less of a drag on US growth and therefore increased confidence in the US economy being reflected in a stronger dollar. The most recent UK reduction in interest rates was done in co-ordination with major central banks in recognition that a monetary stimulus was needed to ward off a possible world-wide recession resulting from the credit crisis and at the same time provide a boost to share prices. US and euro interest

rates were also reduced by 50 basis points to leave interest rates at 1.5 per cent and 3.75 per cent respectively. US growth prospects were further re-inforced by a further 50 basis points reduction in interest rates in late October to 1 per cent.

OUTPUT

Negative growth from contraction in services, construction and industrial output

GDP growth in 2008 quarter three was estimated to have fallen by 0.5 per cent, a deceleration from zero per cent growth in the previous quarter. On an annual basis growth was 0.3 per cent, down markedly from 1.6 per cent growth in the previous quarter.

Construction activity weakened further in quarter three compared with the previous quarter. Construction output is estimated to have fallen by 0.8 per cent, following a fall of 0.5 per cent in the previous quarter. There were decreases in nearly all new work categories but the decline was driven primarily by falls in new private housing, Comparing the quarter on the same quarter a year ago, construction output slowed to growth of 0.7 per cent from 2 per cent growth in the previous quarter (**Figure 3**).

External surveys pointed to sharp declines in housing activity in quarter three – attributing this to a combination of a slowing housing market and lack of availability of debt finance. The CIPS/ Markit UK construction PMI (Purchasing Managers Index) reported that total construction contracted at record pace in the third quarter to a headline balance of 38.7 from 42.9 in the second quarter. The Royal Institute of Chartered Surveyors (RICS) construction survey for 2008 quarter three reported that construction workloads declined for the second successive quarter and at a faster pace – with the net balance falling to minus 38 from minus 19 in the previous quarter.

Total output from the production industries decelerated further in quarter three. Output fell by 1 per cent following a decrease of 0.7 per cent in quarter two. On an annual basis, output contracted by 1.9 per cent, compared to a contraction of 1.1 per cent in the previous quarter.

The weakness in total production was mainly driven by the deterioration in the output of the manufacturing industries. Manufacturing output fell by 1 per cent in the third quarter, a weakening from the 0.9 per cent contraction in the second quarter.

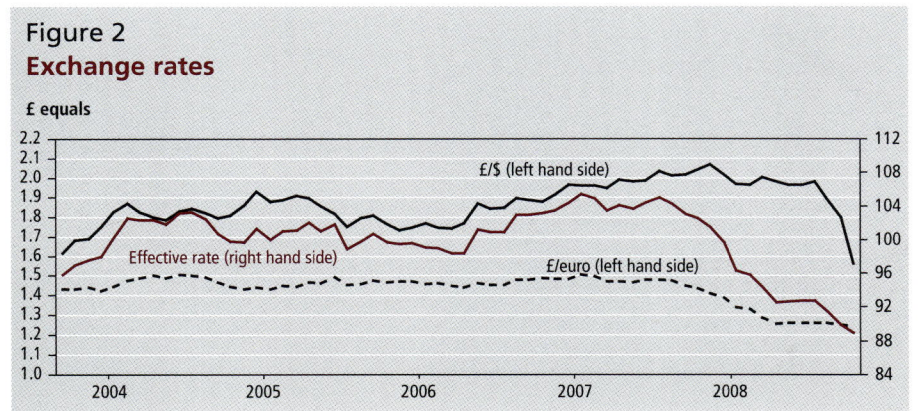

Figure 2
Exchange rates

£ equals

Figure 3
Construction output

Percentage growth

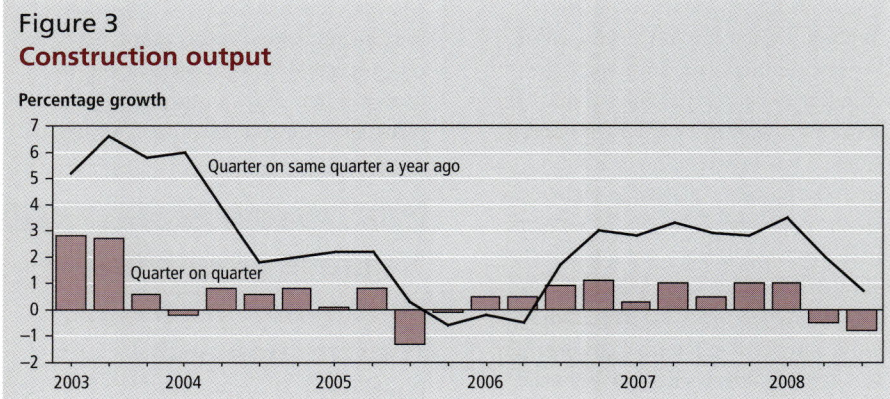

Figure 4
Manufacturing output

Percentage growth

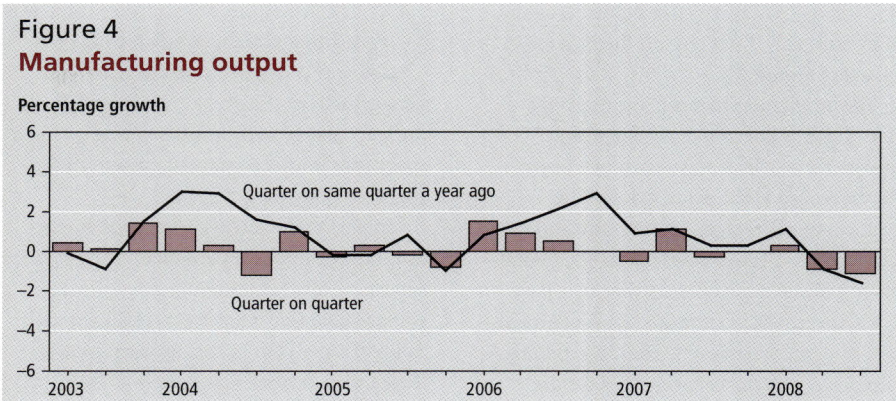

On an annual basis, manufacturing output fell by 1.6 per cent, from a 0.9 per cent decrease in the second quarter (**Figure 4**).

The weakening in total production in quarter three compared with the previous quarter was also to a lesser extent driven by weakness in the output of the electricity, gas and water supply and mining and quarrying industries where output fell by 0.4 per cent and 1.4 per cent respectively. This compares with virtually flat growth recorded for both in the second quarter. On an annual basis, electricity, gas and water supply output registered stagnant growth following 2 per cent growth in the previous quarter. The output of the mining and quarrying industries contracted by 6.7 per cent compared to a fall of 5.9 per cent in the previous quarter.

Production growth has generally been weak in the last couple of years, mainly due to weakness in manufacturing for most of that period, and a contraction in mining and quarrying output, offset through some of this period by relatively strong electricity, gas and water supplies industry output. Manufacturing output has displayed volatility in the recent past. There was a modest pick up in manufacturing output in the first quarter of 2008 but this appears not to have been sustained in subsequent quarters.

The output of the agriculture, forestry and fishing industries increased by 0.5 per

cent in the latest quarter compared with 0.4 per cent growth in the previous quarter. On an annual basis growth was 2.6 per cent, up from 1.8 per cent growth in the previous quarter.

External surveys of manufacturing for 2008 quarter three showed a further deteriorating picture compared with the previous quarter with both weaker domestic and external demand cited as a major factors (**Figure 5**). In the past, it has not been unusual for the path of business indicators and official data to diverge over the short term. These differences happen partly because the series are not measuring exactly the same thing. External surveys measure the direction rather than the magnitude of a change in output and often inquire into expectations rather than actual activity.

The CIPS/ Markit manufacturing PMI indicated a contraction in the latest quarter; the headline index fell further below the no change 50.0 mark to 43.5 from 48.5 in quarter two. The CBI in its 2008 quarter three Industrial Trends survey reported a weakening in its total order books with the balance at minus 39 in the third quarter, compared with minus 8 in the second quarter. The BCC in its 2008 quarter three survey reported alarming results with results pointing to the UK being in recession; the balances for home sales dropped by 10 points to minus 13 and the balance for home orders fell by 12 points to minus 17.

The service sector, the largest part of the UK economy, which has in the past driven UK economic expansion has made a negative contribution to growth in the latest quarter. Services output growth contracted in quarter three accelerating the slowdown of the earlier three quarters.

Services output declined by 0.5 per cent in 2008 quarter three, a deceleration from somewhat negligible growth of 0.2 per cent in the previous quarter but a marked slowdown from a recent high of 1.2 per cent recorded in 2007 quarter one (**Figure 6**). On an annual basis, services output expanded by 0.7 per cent, down from 2.2 per cent in the second quarter.

Declines in growth were recorded in most sectors. The largest contribution to the deceleration in services output in quarter three came from distribution, hotels and catering where output fell by 1.9 per cent following growth of 0.2 per cent in quarter two. On an annual basis, growth fell by 1.4 per cent following a rise of 1.2 per cent in the previous quarter. Output of the transport, storage and communication sector weakened with growth falling by 0.6 per cent after increasing by 1 per cent in quarter two. On an annual basis, growth rose by 1.2 per cent in quarter three, a slowdown from growth of 1.8 per cent in the previous quarter. Business services and

Figure 5
External manufacturing

Balances

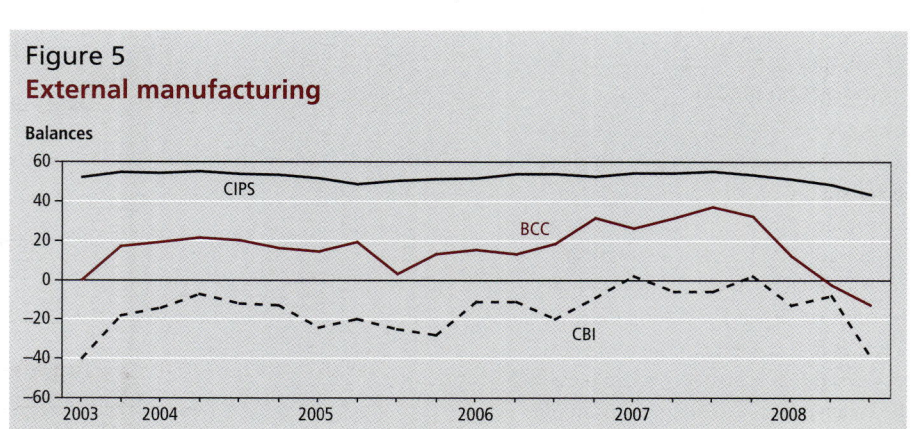

Figure 6
Services output

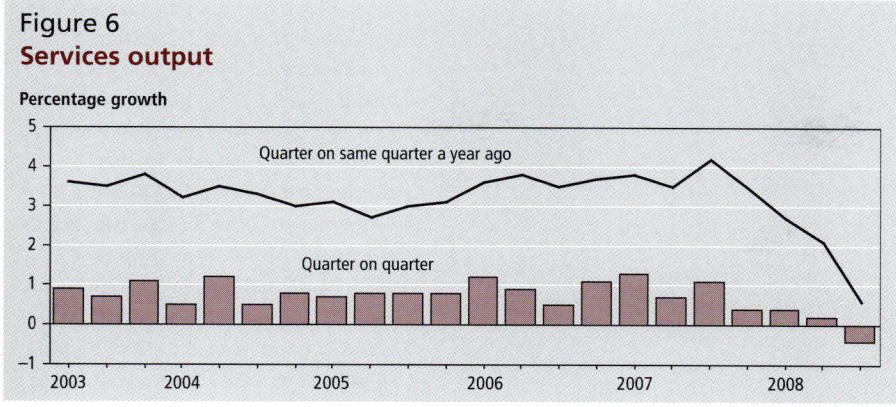

Percentage growth

Quarter on same quarter a year ago

Quarter on quarter

Figure 7
External services

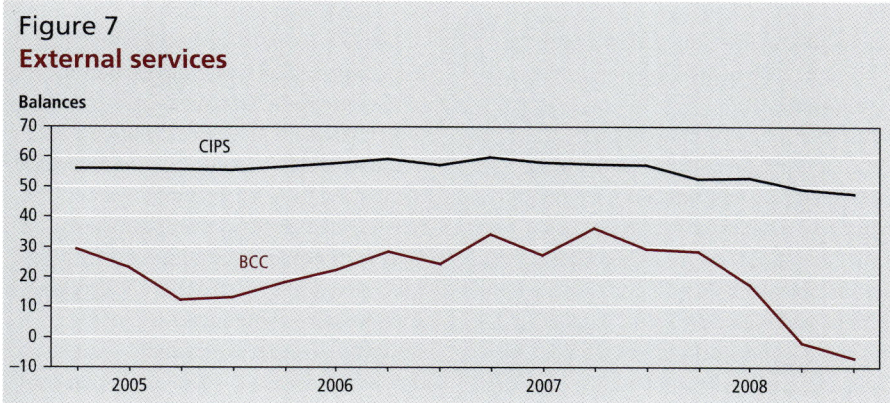

Balances

CIPS

BCC

finance output also decreased, by 0.3 per cent – the first decline since 2002 quarter one – from virtually flat growth in quarter two. On an annual basis, growth was 1.1 per cent, down significantly from 3.2 per cent growth in the second quarter. These decreases were offset by moderate growth in government and other services output of 0.4 per cent in quarter three, up from 0.2 per cent growth in the previous quarter. Growth was 1.2 per cent on the year, marginally down from 1.3 per cent growth in quarter two.

The external surveys on services showed a bleak picture of service sector activity in 2008 quarter three. The CIPS/Markit services PMI survey pointed to a deteriorating picture of service sector activity. The average headline index in 2008 quarter three fell further to 47.5 from 49.1 in quarter two. It should be noted that the CIPS survey has a narrow coverage of the distribution and government sectors.

The CBI and BCC also painted a generally weak picture of service sector activity (**Figure 7**). The latest CBI service sector survey in August reported that for consumer services, volume of business was broadly flat at plus 2 although an improvement from the minus 44 of the previous survey in June. In contrast, volumes for business and professional services, deteriorated at a record pace with the balance reaching minus 31 from plus

10 in the previous survey. The BCC survey for 2008 quarter three recorded alarming declines. The net balance for home sales declined 5 points to minus 7 and the net balance for home orders dropped 6 points to minus 13.

EXPENDITURE

Consumers' spending contracts

Household consumption expenditure decelerated markedly in 2008 quarter two from the previous quarter. Household spending fell by 0.1 per cent compared to an increase of 0.8 per cent in the previous quarter. Compared with the same quarter a year ago, growth was 2.5 per cent, down from 3.6 per cent in the previous quarter (**Figure 8**). Lower spending was

primarily driven by a fall in durable goods and services expenditure. This was offset by fairly strong growth in semi-durable goods and non-durable goods expenditure.

The weakening in consumer expenditure in quarter two may mainly appear to reflect the continued impact of the financial turbulence in the UK economy with pressures on real disposable income arising from modest wage growth coupled with higher inflation, particularly from higher fuel, utility and food prices. Indicators for consumer expenditure appear to be on the downside in quarter three.

One key indicator of household expenditure is retail sales. Retail sales growth continued its slowdown in 2008 quarter three from the previous quarter with retail sales volume growing by a negligible 0.1 per cent, down from 0.5 per cent growth in quarter two. One reason perhaps for the slower growth in retail sales may have been due to the price deflator (that is, shop prices) where discounting appears not to be prevalent or widespread as was the case in quarter two. The price deflator rose on average by 1.2 per cent in quarter three compared with an average fall of 0.1 per cent in the previous quarter, further compounding the pressures on household disposable income.

Retail sales figures are published on a monthly basis and the latest available figures for September 2008 showed a virtually stagnant picture compared with the previous month (**Figure 9**). In the three months to September the volume of retail sales rose by just 0.1 per cent compared with a decrease of 0.9 per cent in the three months to August. On an annual basis in September, growth in the latest three months growth compared with the same three months a year ago was 2.3 per cent, slightly down from 2.4 per cent growth in August.

Retail sales can be disaggregated into 'predominantly food' and 'predominantly non-food' sectors. In the three months to

Figure 8
Household demand

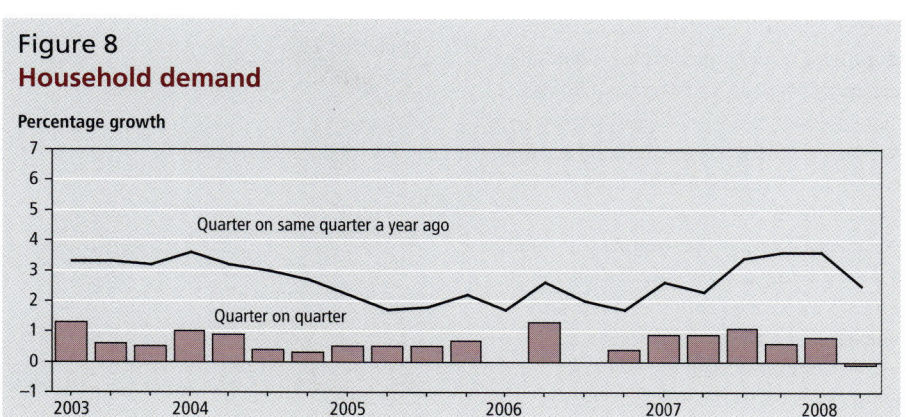

Percentage growth

Quarter on same quarter a year ago

Quarter on quarter

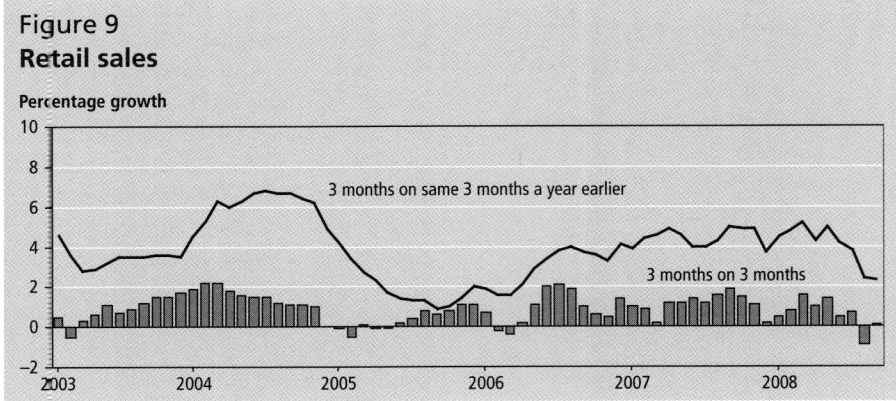

Figure 9
Retail sales

Percentage growth

September 2008, the slowdown in retail sales was driven by continued weakness in the 'predominantly food-stores' sector offset by modest growth in the 'predominantly non-food stores' sector. Growth in 'predominantly food stores' fell by 1.1 per cent compared with a fall of 1.3 per cent in the three months to August.

In contrast, growth in 'predominantly non-food stores' rose by 0.6 per cent in the three months to September, reversing the contraction of 0.8 per cent in the three months to August. Within this sector growth was primarily driven by 'non-store retailing and repair' which grew by 2.6 per cent, an acceleration from 1 per cent growth in the previous three months. Growth was also led by 'textile, clothing and footwear stores' which rose by 2.1 per cent following an increase of 1 per cent in August and 'other stores' which grew by 1.1 percent, rebounding on a fall of 1.3 per cent in August. This was offset by a decline in growth in 'Non-specialised stores' where growth fell by 1.4 per cent from a 0.6 per cent decrease in August. Household goods stores also showed weakness with volume of sales falling by 0.3 per cent compared to a contraction of 2.4 per cent in the three months to August.

It should be noted that household consumption accounts for a much broader range of spending than just retail sales. For instance, household purchases of services, motor vehicles and housing (imputed rents) are not included in retail sales. Since the beginning of 2006 quarter two, retail sales generally have grown faster than household consumption as a whole. However, the gap appears to have narrowed in 2008 quarter two and may conceivably be minimal in quarter three.

External surveys for retail sales presented a deteriorating picture of growth in 2008 quarter three compared to the previous quarter. The CBI reported an average balance of minus 32 in the latest quarter, from minus 16 in the previous quarter. The

BRC reported average growth of 1.4 per cent in 2008 quarter three, down from 2.6 per cent in 2008 quarter two on a total sales basis (**Figure 10**).

Another indicator of household consumption expenditure is borrowing. Household consumption has risen faster than disposable income in recent years as the household sector has become a considerable net borrower and therefore accumulated high debt levels. Bank of England data on stocks of household debt outstanding to banks and building societies shows household debt at unprecedented levels relative to disposable income. Until recently, this borrowing has fuelled consumption, but indicators appear to suggest this to be less so in the latest two quarters.

There are two channels of borrowing available to households: i) secured lending, usually on homes; and ii) unsecured lending, for example on credit cards. The impact of the credit squeeze continued to have a substantial impact in quarter three. According to the Bank of England's Credit Conditions Survey, lending conditions were tightened further in quarter three, that is, by applying stringent credit-scoring criteria and by decreasing maximum loan-to-value (LTV) ratios – with lenders reporting that they had reduced the availability of both secured and unsecured lending to households. The tightening was driven by

concerns about the economic outlook and falling collateral values.

Another indicator highlighting the downside risks to consumer expenditure is described by Bank of England lending figures. There were signs of further slowdown with total lending growing by approximately £5 billion in the two months July to August, down from around £15 billion in the second quarter. Over the same period, lending secured on dwellings fell to around £3 billion from around £12 billion in the second quarter. Unsecured lending grew roughly by £2 billion, down from £3 billion in the second quarter.

The slowdown in secured lending may have impacted on house prices in terms of lower growth. Nationwide and Halifax both reported house prices falling in quarter three by around 5 per cent, broadly unchanged from the previous quarter. The housing market plays a major influence on consumer expenditure patterns. Firstly, as a barometer of confidence in the economy and therefore a willingness to spend; secondly, in terms of demand it creates for household goods via house purchases; and thirdly, household expenditure may be linked to household equity withdrawal (HEW) – slower house price growth can signify lower equity growth and therefore decreasing purchasing power. The recent slowdown in house prices and the housing market generally may have affected all three of the above, compounded by the credit squeeze, rising unemployment and lower household income.

There are a number of unknowns in the third quarter in terms of determinants of consumer expenditure. First is the savings ratio: In the second quarter, the weakness in household expenditure may have been partly attributable to the savings ratio - with signs of a retrenchment amongst households reflected in a modest rise in the savings ratio of 0.4 per cent, but it also could have been a reflection and symptom of the spending pressures faced

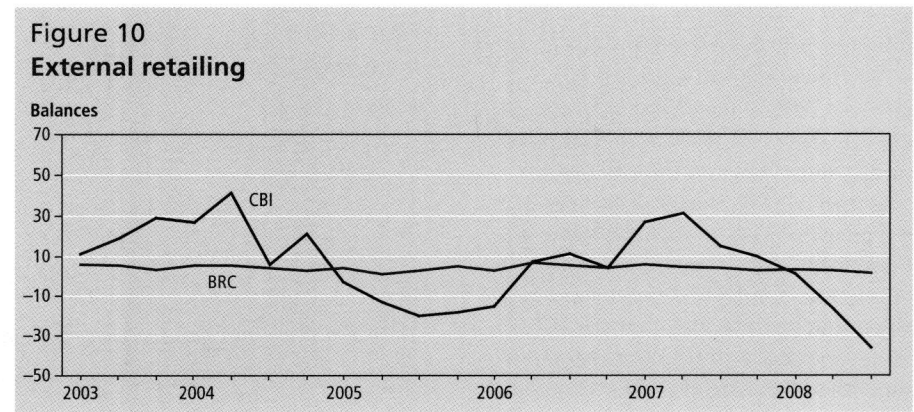

Figure 10
External retailing

Balances

by households'. In the third quarter, the question is what scope there is for a further draw down or consolidation in household savings? Second, the recent fall in oil prices may play a significant factor in consumer expenditure not only in terms of boosting disposable income but also in terms of consumers' being able to switch to durable goods expenditure. Third, consumer expenditure is determined by the 'confidence' factor and this in turn will be affected by the situation in regards to labour market activity and the growth in real disposable incomes.

BUSINESS DEMAND

Business investment contracts

Total investment fell by 2.8 per cent in 2008 quarter two compared with a fall of 2 per cent in the previous quarter. On an annual basis, total investment fell by 2.1 per cent, reversing positive growth of 0.3 per cent in the previous quarter. The decrease in total investment was due to both business and dwelling investment falling over the quarter (**Figure 11**).

Business investment continued to contract in the latest quarter. Business investment decreased by 1 per cent in the latest quarter, compared with 1.9 per cent growth in the previous quarter. On an annual basis, business investment grew by 1.2 per cent, a slowdown from 3.1 per cent growth in 2008 quarter one.

Business investment could have decreased for a number of reasons. Firstly, increased uncertainty and pessimism in regards to global and domestic demand, may have deterred investment; secondly, the downturn in investment could have come on the back of lower corporate profits; thirdly, the weakness in the equity market in recent quarters may have constrained revenue generation and hence investment; and last but not least, the general weakness in the property market in terms of lower price growth may have inhibited investment spending.

Evidence on investment intentions from the latest BCC and CBI surveys painted a picture of weakness. According to the latest quarterly BCC survey, the balance of manufacturing firms planning to increase investment in plant and machinery dropped by 6 points to minus 4. The CBI's Quarterly Industrial Survey in 2008 quarter three also reported a bleaker investment picture, with the investment balance of plant and machinery weakening to minus 38 from minus 24 in the previous quarter.

GOVERNMENT DEMAND

Government expenditure moderates

Government final consumption expenditure slowed in 2008 quarter two. Growth registered a fairly modest 0.5 per cent compared with growth of 1 per cent in the previous quarter. On an annual basis, growth was 2.1 per cent, similar to the rate in the previous quarter (**Figure 12**).

Public sector finances deteriorate

The latest figures on the public sector finances to September 2008 illustrated a weakening position. The figures showed a higher current budget deficit together with an increased net borrowing situation – reflecting government expenditure continuing to exceed tax revenues. In the financial year 2008/09 to date, the current budget was in deficit by £25.5 billion; this compares with a budget deficit of £13.1 billion in the same period of 2007/08. Public sector net borrowing in the financial year 2008/09 to date was £37.6 billion; this compares with net borrowing of £21.5 billion in the same period of 2007/08. Slower growths in current receipts were exceeded by a larger increase in the rate of current expenditure, particularly on capital

projects – resulting in both a higher budget deficit and net borrowing.

Since net borrowing became positive in 2002, following the current budget moving from surplus into deficit, net debt as a proportion of annual GDP has risen steadily. Public sector net debt in September 2008 was 43.4 per cent of GDP (including Northern Rock), up from 42.7 per cent in August 2008. In the full financial year 2006/07, net debt as a percentage of GDP was 42.8 per cent.

TRADE AND THE BALANCE OF PAYMENTS

Current account deficit widens; goods trade deficit narrows slightly in quarter two

The publication of the latest quarterly Balance of Payments figures shows that the current account deficit widened in 2008 quarter two to £11.0 billion, from a revised deficit of £5.5 billion in the previous quarter (**Figure 13**). As a proportion of GDP, the deficit increased to 3 per cent of GDP from 1.5 per cent in 2008 quarter one. The widening in the current account deficit in 2008 quarter two was due to a lower surplus on income, partially offset by a fall in the deficit in current transfers. The surplus on income decreased by £6.0 billion to £4.5 billion and the deficit

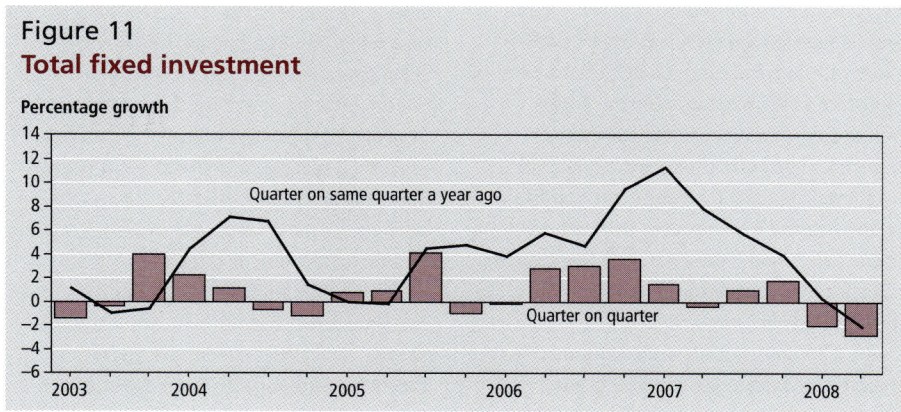

Figure 11
Total fixed investment

Percentage growth

Quarter on same quarter a year ago

Quarter on quarter

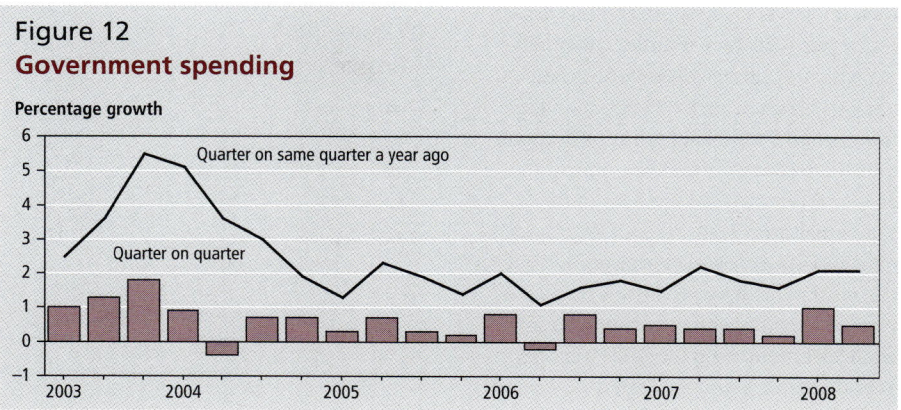

Figure 12
Government spending

Percentage growth

Quarter on same quarter a year ago

Quarter on quarter

Figure 13
Balance of payments

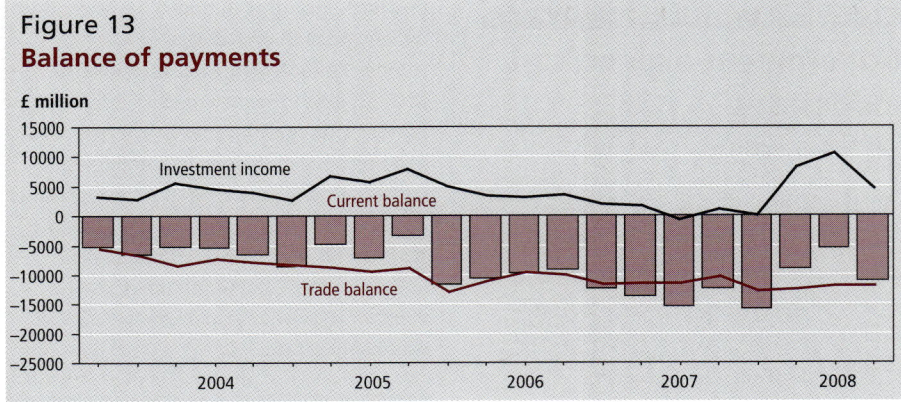

£ million

in current transfers fell by £0.4 billion to £3.5 billion. The lower surplus on income was mainly due to higher interest payments from UK securities dealers combined with lower losses recorded by foreign banks with UK operations.

The run of current account deficits since 1998 reflects the sustained deterioration in the trade balance. The UK has traditionally run a surplus on the trade in services, complemented by a surplus in investment income, but this has been more than offset by the growing deficit in trade in goods partly due to the UK's appetite for cheaper imports.

The figures in 2008 quarter two showed a continuation in the goods trade deficit but a slight narrowing from quarter one. The goods trade deficit was £23.1 billion in 2008 quarter one, down from a deficit of £23.2 billion in the previous quarter. Overall, there was a fall in imports together with stagnant exports – leading to a fall in the total trade balance to a deficit of £12.0 billion in 2008 quarter two from £12.1 billion in quarter one. Over the quarter in terms of growth, total exports flat and total imports fell by 0.5 per cent. Exports of goods grew by 1 per cent while goods imports fell by 0.8 per cent. Services exports fell by 2.7 per cent and services imports decreased by 3.3 per cent.

According to the latest trade figures, the UK's deficit in trade in goods and services widened to £13.9 billion in the three months to August, from £11.3 billion in the previous three months - driven by the widening of the goods trade deficit to £24.4 billion from £22.5 billion in the three months to May, and from a decrease in the surplus in the trade in services to £10.5 billion from £11.3 billion in the three months to May. In terms of growth, total exports in volume terms grew by 1.6 per cent in the three months to August compared with the previous three months while total imports grew by 2.2 per cent over the same period.

External surveys on exports reported a weakening picture in quarter three. The BCC reported that the export sales net balance dropped 25 points to plus 3. The CBI quarterly survey reported the order books balance at minus 32.

LABOUR MARKET

Labour market activity slowdown deepens

The labour market in the latest reference period showed further signs of deterioration, but overall, still reflected a fairly buoyant picture – with relatively high levels of employment and low levels of unemployment seen throughout 2007 and early 2008. However, there was a broader weakening in indicators of the labour market in the latest reference period, reflecting the lagged effect of the slowdown in the economy which began in the fourth quarter of 2007 and which has markedly deteriorated in subsequent quarters.

The latest figures from the Labour Force Survey (LFS) pertain to the three-month period up to August 2008. Most indicators appear on the downside. There was a fall in both the number of people in employment and the employment rate. The number of unemployed people and the unemployment rate increased. The number of inactive people of working age increased but the inactivity rate was unchanged. Vacancies

fell. Growth in average earnings (both including and excluding bonuses) fell; overall, average earnings remain subdued with weak real-wage growth.

Near record levels of employment continue despite the sharp fall in employment in the current period, compared with the previous quarter. The number of people in employment decreased by 122,000 in the three months to August – the biggest fall since the beginning of 1993 - but rose 199,000 on a year earlier. The current working-age employment rate was 74.4 per cent in the three months to August 2008, down 0.4 percentage points from the three months to May 2008 and down 0.1 percentage point from a year earlier – leaving the employment level at 29.42 million. Unemployment levels on the other hand rose and for the sixth month in a row. The number of unemployed people increased by 164,000 in the three months to August 2008 – the fastest increase for 17 years – and up 146,000 from a year earlier, leaving the unemployment level at 1.79 million. The unemployment rate also rose, to 5.7 per cent in the three months to August 2008, up 0.5 percentage points from the three months to May 2008 and up from 0.4 percentage points a year earlier (**Figure 14**).

Looking at a detailed level, the decrease in the employment level was mainly driven by employees and to a lesser extent in self-employment. Employees fell by 52,000 while the self-employed decreased by 31,000. In terms of full and part-time workers, the numbers of people in full-time employment fell by 152,000 while the number of people in part-time employment increased by 30,000.

Workforce jobs increases

According to employer surveys' there were 31.68 million workforce jobs in June 2008, up 26,000 over the quarter and up 142,000 on a year earlier. The largest quarterly contribution to the increase came from education, health and public

Figure 14
Employment and unemployment

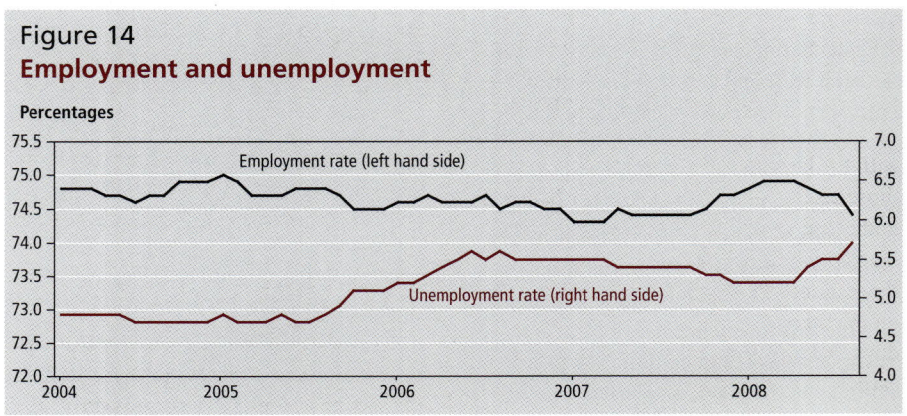

Percentages

admin (up 27,000), followed by agriculture, forestry and fishing (up 15,000). This was offset by decreases across a number of sectors with the largest decrease in distribution, hotels and restaurants (down 11,000) followed by manufacturing (down 10,000). The largest contribution to the increase over the year came from education, health and public administration (up 43,000) followed by finance and business services (up, 40,000), partially offset by manufacturing (down 47,000).

Claimant count increases further

The claimant count measures the number of people claiming the Jobseeker's Allowance. The latest figures for September 2008 showed the claimant count level rose by 31,800 – the eighth consecutive monthly increase. On a year earlier the claimant count level increased by 104,900 to reach a level of 939,900. The claimant count rate in September 2008 was 2.9 per cent, up 0.1 percentage point from the previous month and up 0.3 percentage points from a year earlier.

Vacancies showed another big fall

The number of vacancies fell further compared to the previous quarter reflecting weakening demand conditions in the UK economy. Job vacancies fell by 40,000 and were down 62,000 from the same period a year earlier reaching a level of 608,000 vacancies in the three months to September 2008.

Inactivity level increases

In level terms, the number of economically inactive people of working age increased by 16,000 over the quarter but fell by 74,000 over the year to reach 7.89 million in the three months to August 2008. The largest rise in level of inactivity was recorded for those categorised as 'student' (up 66,000) followed by the 'long-term sick' category (up 18,000). This was partially offset by a number of decreases, with the largest fall in inactivity amongst those categorised as 'looking after family/ home' (down 42,000). The working-age inactivity rate was 20.9 per cent in the three months to August 2008, unchanged on the three months to May 2008 but down 0.3 percentage points from a year earlier

Average earnings growth subdued

Growth in whole-economy average earnings showed a relatively muted picture in the three months to August 2008. Average earnings including bonuses, increased by 3.4 per cent, down 0.1 percentage point from the previous month. Average earnings excluding bonuses rose by 3.6 per cent, also down 0.1 percentage point from the previous period. Public and private sector earnings grew modestly in the latest month. In terms of the public and private sector split, average earnings (excluding bonuses) grew in parity in the latest month. Public sector earnings growth was 3.6 per cent, down 0.1 percentage points from the previous month. Private sector earnings also grew by 3.6 per cent, down 0.1 percentage point from the previous month.

Overall, the numbers still point to a fairly buoyant labour market, with employment at high levels and unemployment at a fairly stable level. However, the slowing economy is starting to show a deeper turning point in labour market activity, particularly in terms of declining employment growth and larger increases in unemployment levels. Average earnings show stable but fairly modest growth, consistent with softening in labour market activity and increase in supply in the labour force.

PRICES

Producer output and input price pressures persist in quarter three

Industrial input and output prices are an indication of inflationary pressures in the economy. During the third quarter of 2008, output and input prices continued to remain elevated and broadly unchanged from the second quarter – a sign that the rise in world commodity prices was continuing to exert considerable influence in generating UK inflation through higher product prices. In the latest quarter, there appeared signs of easing in input price growth compared to marginally faster growth in output price inflation – which possibly suggests that firms were intent on maintaining their profit margins by passing on the relatively high input costs to customers.

Input prices on average rose by 28.2 per cent in 2008 quarter three. This compares with 29.8 per cent in 2008 quarter two. On the core measure, which strips out the effect of food, beverages, tobacco and petroleum

prices, input prices on average rose by 20.7 per cent in 2008 quarter three (12 month non-seasonally adjusted growth), an acceleration from growth of 18.8 per cent in the previous quarter. The strength in input prices continued to be generated mainly by fuel and imported food materials prices which rose on average by 40 per cent and 25 per cent respectively in quarter three.

Output prices grew on average by 9.2 per cent in 2008 quarter three, a marginal increase from growth of 8.8 per cent in the previous quarter. The underlying picture also suggests inflationary pressures. On the core measure which excludes food, beverages, tobacco and petroleum, producer output prices rose by 5.7 per cent in 2008 quarter three, up from 5.2 per cent in the previous quarter. The main contributions to the increase in output prices were provided by rises in petroleum products and food prices which grew on average by 31.2 per cent and 13.2 per cent respectively in quarter three. Higher output and input prices appear to be fuelling consumer price inflation.

Consumer prices increases further and considerably above target

Growth in the consumer prices index (CPI) – the Government's target measure of inflation – increased further in September to 5.2 per cent, up from 4.7 per cent in August and considerably above the Government's 2 per cent inflation target (**Figure 15**).

The largest upward pressure on the CPI annual rate came from housing and household services because of rises in average gas and electricity bills this year compared with falls last year. Within this division there was also a small upward effect from materials for maintenance and repair, principally from paint.

There were further large upward pressures from:

- recreation and culture where, overall, prices rose by more than a year ago. The pressures came mainly from computer games, data processing equipment, admission to live music events and foreign holidays
- clothing and footwear where prices rose by more than a year ago, particularly for men's outerwear
- air and sea fares falling at the end of the summer by less than a year ago. With air fares, the upward pressure came from long-haul routes partially offset by a downward effect from European flights. The sea fares effect came from international routes

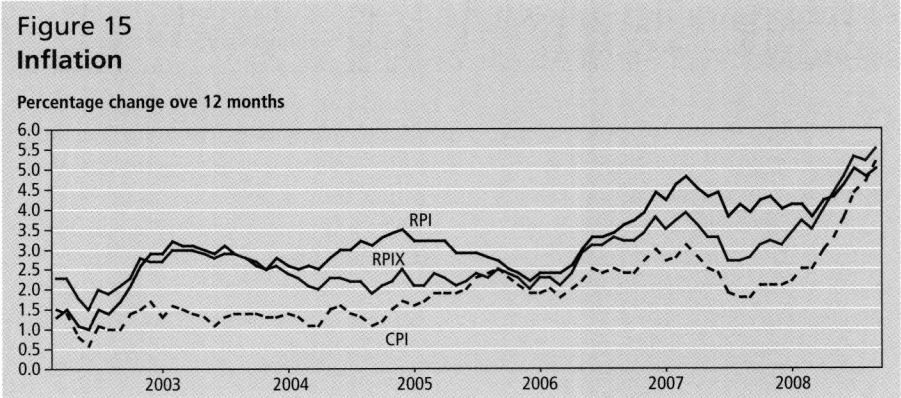

Figure 15
Inflation

Percentage change ove 12 months

The largest downward pressure on the CPI annual rate came from food and non-alcoholic beverages with the largest single effect coming from shop-bought milk whose prices were little changed this year but rose by 4 pence a pint a year ago. There was also a large downward effect from fruit and smaller effects from bread and cereals, oils and fats, and mineral waters, soft drinks and juices. These were partially offset by a large upward effect from meat, particularly bacon.

There were also large downward effects from:

- second-hand cars and fuels and lubricants, with prices of both groups falling by more than a year ago. The average price of petrol fell by 1.7 pence per litre between August and September this year, to stand at 111.6 pence, compared with a fall of 0.9 pence last year. Diesel prices fell by 2.3 pence per litre this year compared with a fall of 0.1 pence last year
- education, where private school fees rose by less than a year ago

Retail Prices Index (RPI) inflation rose to 5.0 per cent in September, up from 4.8 per cent in August. The main factors affecting the CPI also affected the RPI. Additionally, there was a large downward contribution from housing with the main effect coming from house depreciation partially offset by buildings insurance. Depreciation and buildings insurance are excluded from the CPI.

RPIX inflation – the all items RPI excluding mortgage interest payments – was 5.5 per cent in September, up from 5.2 per cent in August.

Independent forecasts

October 2008

UK forecasts

The tables below supplement the Economic Review by providing a forward-looking view of the UK economy. The tables shows the average and range of independent forecasts for 2008 and 2009 and are extracted from HM Treasury's Forecasts for the UK Economy.

2008

	Average	Lowest	Highest
GDP growth (per cent)	1.1	0.6	1.6
Inflation rate (Q4, per cent)			
CPI	4.5	2.9	5.0
RPI	4.6	3.4	5.9
Claimant count (Q4, million)	0.97	0.90	1.10
Current account (£ billion)	−42.2	−67.4	−21.4
Public Sector Net Borrowing (2007–08, £ billion)	57.2	31.0	120.0

2009

	Average	Lowest	Highest
GDP growth (per cent)	0.1	−1.9	3.0
Inflation rate (Q4, per cent)			
CPI	2.1	1.0	4.4
RPI	2.0	0.3	4.5
Claimant count (Q4, million)	1.24	0.83	1.70
Current account (£ billion)	−42.0	−86.4	−14.1
Public Sector Net Borrowing (2009–10, £ billion)	68.0	30.0	90.0

Notes

Forecast for the UK economy gives more detailed forecasts, and is published monthly by HM Treasury. It is available on the Treasury's website at: www.hm-treasury.gov.uk/economic_data_and_tools/data_index.cfm

Selected world forecasts

The tables below supplement the Economic Review by providing a forward-looking view of the world economy. The tables show forecasts for a range of economic indicators taken from *Economic Outlook* (June 2008), published by OECD (Organisation for Economic Co-operation and Development).

2008

	US	Japan	Euro area	Total OECD
Real GDP growth (per cent)	1.2	1.7	1.7	1.8
Consumer price (percentage change from previous year)	3.2	0.9	3.4	3.0
Unemployment rate (per cent of the labour force)	5.4	3.8	7.2	5.7
Current account (as a percentage of GDP)	−5.0	4.4	0.1	−1.3
Fiscal balance (as a percentage of GDP)	−5.2	−1.6	−1.0	−2.8

2009

	US	Japan	Euro area	Total OECD
Real GDP growth (per cent)	1.1	1.5	1.4	1.7
Consumer price (percentage change from previous year)	2.0	0.4	2.4	2.1
Unemployment rate (per cent of the labour force)	6.1	3.8	7.4	6.0
Current account (as a percentage of GDP)	−4.4	4.4	0.0	−1.1
Fiscal balance (as a percentage of GDP)	−4.4	−2.5	−0.8	−2.5

Notes

The OECD *Economic Outlook* is published bi-annually. Further information about this publication can be found at www.oecd.org/eco/Economic_Outlook

Key indicators

The data in this table support the Economic review by providing some of the latest estimates of Key indicators.

Seasonally adjusted unless otherwise stated

	Source CDID	2006	2007	2008 Q1	2008 Q2	2008 Q3	2008 Jul	2008 Aug	2008 Sep
GDP growth – chained volume measures (CVM)									
Gross domestic product at market prices	ABMI	2.8	3.0	0.3	0.0	–0.5	..	..	..
Output growth – chained volume measures (CVM)									
Gross value added (GVA) at basic prices	ABMM	2.9	3.0	0.3	0.0	–0.5	..	..	..
Industrial production	CKYW	0.7	0.4	–0.5	–0.7	–1.0	–0.5	–0.5	..
Manufacturing	CKYY	1.8	0.7	0.3	–0.9	–1.1	–0.2	–0.5	..
Construction	GDQB	1.0	2.9	1.0	–0.5	–0.8	..	..	..
Services	GDQS	3.7	3.7	0.4	0.2	–0.4	..	..	..
Oil and gas extraction	CKZO	–8.9	–2.5	–3.6	–0.1	..	–4.4	–1.2	..
Electricity, gas and water supply	CKYZ	–0.6	1.2	–2.1	–0.1	–1.1	0.9	–1.7	..
Business services and finance	GDQN	5.9	5.9	0.6	0.2	–0.4	..	..	..
Household demand									
Retail sales volume growth	EAPS	3.2	4.3	1.5	0.5	0.1	0.9	1.1	–0.4
Household final consumption expenditure growth (CVM)	ABJR	2.0	3.0	0.8	–0.1	..	..	..	..
GB new registrations of cars (thousands)[1]	BCGT	2,340	2,390	675	557	542	151	63	329
Labour market[2,3]									
Employment: 16 and over (thousands)	MGRZ	29,030	29,222	29,499	29,505	..	29,419	..	..
Employment rate: working age (%)	MGSU	74.6	74.6	74.8	74.7	..	74.4	..	..
Workforce jobs (thousands)	DYDC	31,294	31,536	31,652	31,678	..	..	..	..
Total actual weekly hours of work: all workers (millions)	YBUS	928.5	936.6	948.1	939.9	..	944.2	..	..
Unemployment: 16 and over (thousands)	MGSC	1,669	1,653	1,624	1,685	..	1,792	..	..
Unemployment rate: 16 and over (%)	MGSX	5.4	5.3	5.2	5.4	..	5.7	..	..
Claimant count (thousands)	BCJD	944.7	863.3	796.5	826.5	906.8	872.4	908.1	939.9
Economically active: 16 and over (thousands)	MGSF	30,698	30,875	31,123	31,190	..	31,211	..	..
Economic activity rate: working age (%)	MGSO	78.9	78.9	79.1	79.1	..	79.1	..	..
Economically inactive: working age (thousands)	YBSN	7,859	7,940	7,871	7,872	..	7,886	..	..
Economic inactivity rate: working age (%)	YBTL	21.0	21.1	20.9	20.9	..	20.9	..	..
Vacancies (thousands)	AP2Y	597	658	687	649	608	631	615	608
Redundancies (thousands)	BEAO	138	127	111	127	..	147	..	..
Productivity and earnings annual growth									
GB average earnings (including bonuses)[3]	LNNC	..	..	4.0	3.5	..	3.5	3.4	..
GB average earnings (excluding bonuses)[3]	JQDY	..	..	3.8	3.7	..	3.7	3.6	..
Whole economy productivity (output per worker)	A4YN	..	..	0.7	0.2	..	..	..	..
Manufacturing productivity (output per job)	LOUV	..	..	..	..	..	0.4	0.2	..
Unit wage costs: whole economy	LOJE	..	..	1.8	2.4	..	..	..	..
Unit wage costs: manufacturing	LOJF	..	..	..	..	..	2.4	2.6	..
Business demand									
Business investment growth (CVM)	NPEL	–7.2	9.8	–1.9	–1.0	..	..	..	..
Government demand									
Government final consumption expenditure growth	NMRY	1.6	1.8	1.0	0.5	..	..	..	..
Prices (12–monthly percentage change – except oil prices)[1]									
Consumer prices index	D7G7	2.3	2.3	2.4	3.4	4.8	4.4	4.7	5.2
Retail prices index	CZBH	3.2	4.3	4.0	4.4	5.0	5.0	4.8	5.0
Retail prices index (excluding mortgage interest payments)	CDKQ	2.9	3.2	3.5	4.4	5.3	5.3	5.2	5.5
Producer output prices (excluding FBTP)[4,5]		1.8	1.9	2.9	5.2	5.8	6.3	5.6	5.4
Producer input prices[5]		9.5	3.0	20.7	29.9	28.2	31.4	28.8	24.5
Oil price: sterling (£ per barrel)	ETXR	35.93	36.11	48.72	62.35	61.64	67.65	61.11	56.15
Oil price: dollars ($ per barrel)	ETXQ	66.11	72.44	96.47	122.87	116.89	134.52	115.23	100.92

Seasonally adjusted unless otherwise stated

	Source CDID	2006	2007	2008 Q1	2008 Q2	2008 Q3	2008 Jul	2008 Aug	2008 Sep
Financial markets[1]									
Sterling ERI (January 2005=100)	BK67	101.2	103.5	95.6	92.9	91.6	93.2	91.6	89.9
Average exchange rate /US$	AUSS	1.8429	2.0021	1.9780	1.9708	1.8934	1.9880	1.8889	1.7986
Average exchange rate /Euro	THAP	1.4670	1.4619	1.3212	1.2615	1.2586	1.2615	1.2614	1.2531
3–month inter–bank rate	HSAJ	5.26	5.95	5.95	5.88	6.15	5.75	5.70	6.15
Selected retail banks: base rate	ZCMG						5.00	5.00	5.00
3–month interest rate on US Treasury bills	LUST	4.89	3.29	1.36	1.87	0.86	1.67	1.69	0.86
Trade and the balance of payments									
UK balance on trade in goods (£m)	BOKI	−76,312	−89,252	−23,197	−23,140	..	−8,238	−8,198	..
Exports of services (£m)	IKBB	132,749	147,634	39,828	40,065	..	13,014	12,936	..
Non–EU balance on trade in goods (£m)	LGDT	−44,921	−47,788	−12,361	−13,165	..	−4,788	−5,165	..
Non–EU exports of goods (excl oil & erratics)[6]	SHDJ	118.0	116.5	125.7	127.8	..	132.3	122.4	..
Non–EU imports of goods (excl oil & erratics)[6]	SHED	124.4	131.6	133.0	132.4	..	134.8	137.2	..
Non–EU import and price index (excl oil)[6]	LKWQ	103.9	104.2	109.9	113.4	..	113.7	115.4	..
Non–EU export and price index (excl oil)[6]	LKVX	101.5	102.5	106.4	108.1	..	108.2	109.9	..
Monetary conditions/government finances									
Narrow money: notes and coin (year on year percentage growth)[7]	VQUU	5.1	5.8	6.7	5.7	5.1	5.8	5.0	5.1
M4 (year on year percentage growth)	VQJW	13.0	12.7	11.7	11.4	12.4	11.2	11.5	12.4
Public sector net borrowing (£m)[1]	−ANNX	30,327	35,893	−2,232	23,241	14,348	−4,092	10,348	8,092
Net lending to consumers (£m)	RLMH	13,243	13,112	4,286	3,440	..	1,051	1,236	..

External indicators – non–ONS statistics

	Source CDID	2008 Mar	2008 Apr	2008 May	2008 Jun	2008 Jul	2008 Aug	2008 Sep	2008 Oct
Activity and expectations									
CBI output expectations balance[1]	ETCU	18	0	0	2	−7	−13	−16	−31
CBI optimism balance[1]	ETBV		−23			−40			−60
CBI price expectations balance	ETDQ	22	23	29	29	39	31	27	12

Notes: *Source: Office for National Statistics*

1   Not seasonally adjusted.
2   Annual data are the average of the four quarters except for workforce jobs (June).
3   Monthly data for vacancies and average earnings are averages of the three months ending in the month shown. Monthly data for all other series except claimant count are averages of the three months centred on the month shown.
4   FBTP: food, beverages, tobacco and petroleum.
5   Now derived from not seasonally adjusted series; there are no source CDIDs.
6   Volumes, 2003 = 100.
7   Replacement for series M0 which has ceased publication.

Further explanatory notes appear at the end of the Key times series section.

Debra Leaker
Office for National Statistics

FEATURE

Sickness absence from work in the UK

SUMMARY

This article presents sickness absence rates by various personal and labour market characteristics, from the Labour Force Survey, for working-age (men aged 16 to 64 and women aged 16 to 59) employees. It also presents logistic regression analysis, which is a method to combine a range of factors affecting sickness absence to see their effect, and finally looks at other sources of information on sickness absence from work.

In the period July 2007 to June 2008, around 5.8 million scheduled working days were lost to sickness or injury: this accounted for 1.5 per cent of scheduled working days. Women and those working in the public sector are most likely to be absent from work because of sickness or injury.

Direct costs of sickness absence to employers include statutory sick pay, expense of covering absence with temporary staff and lost production. Indirect costs, such as low morale among staff covering for those absent because of sickness and lower customer satisfaction, are harder to measure, but also impact on the overall levels of output. The 2008 Confederation of Business Industry (CBI) report found the direct cost of absence in 2007 was £13.2 billion, around £517 for each employee. The CBI estimates that indirect costs added another £263 for each employee. When these indirect costs are added to the direct costs, the CBI estimates the UK lost £19.9 billion to absence in 2007.

Labour Force Survey

The Labour Force Survey (LFS) is a quarterly sample survey of about 53,000 households living at private addresses in the UK, representing about 0.2 per cent of the population. The survey asks respondents for information on their personal circumstances and labour market status. The survey also collects information on whether a respondent took days off because of sickness or injury in the reference week (usually the week before the survey interview). This allows calculation of an estimate of working days lost because of sickness absence in the reference week. It also allows calculation of a sickness absence rate, the proportion of all working-age employees who took at least one day off due to sickness or injury in the reference week.[1]

These rates do not take account of the total duration of a person's sickness absence, as the use of the reference week means the LFS can only measure sickness absence lasting for a maximum of seven days, including those on long-term sick absence.

Trends in sickness absence rates

Figure 1 shows that sickness absence rates fluctuate throughout the year. They are lowest in July to September and highest in January to March or October to December. Figures presented in the next section combine data from July to September, October to December, January to March and April to June, presenting data from one mid-year to the next.

Figure 2 shows that the sickness absence rate for all employees decreased between the 12 months ending June 2001 and the 12 months ending June 2006. Since this period, sickness absence rates for all working-age employees have remained stable at around 2.5 per cent, which means some 2.5 per cent of working-age employees had at least one day's absence from work in the reference week because of sickness or injury.

Data in the following section are for the period July 2007 to June 2008.

In the twelve months ending June 2008, there were 5.8 million scheduled working days lost to sickness or injury. This accounted for 1.5 per cent of scheduled working days.

Figure 3 shows that the sickness absence rate for women absent from work because of sickness or injury was 2.9

Figure 1
Quarterly sickness absence rates of working-age employees

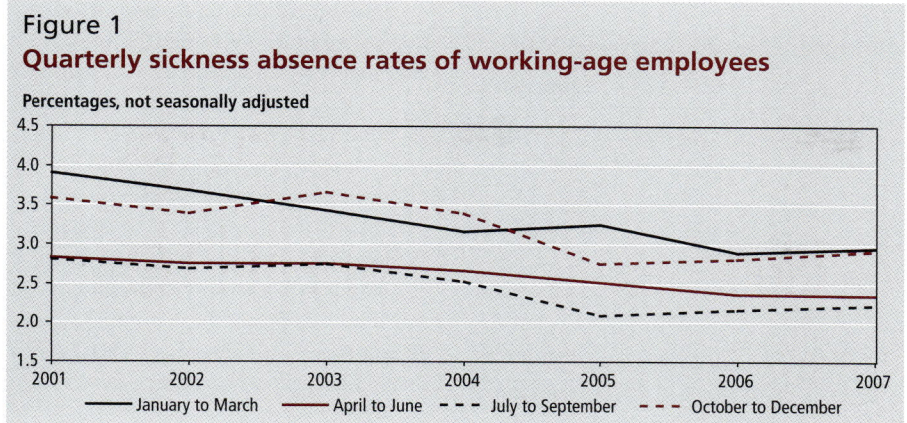

Percentages, not seasonally adjusted

— January to March   — April to June   - - - July to September   - - - October to December

Source: Labour Force Survey

Figure 2
Sickness absence rates of working-age employees[1]

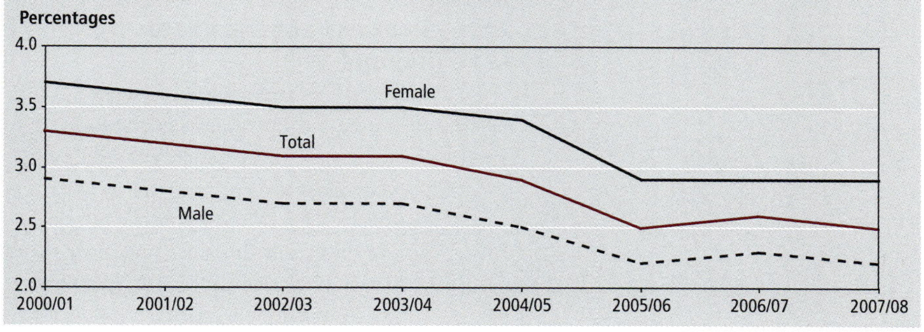

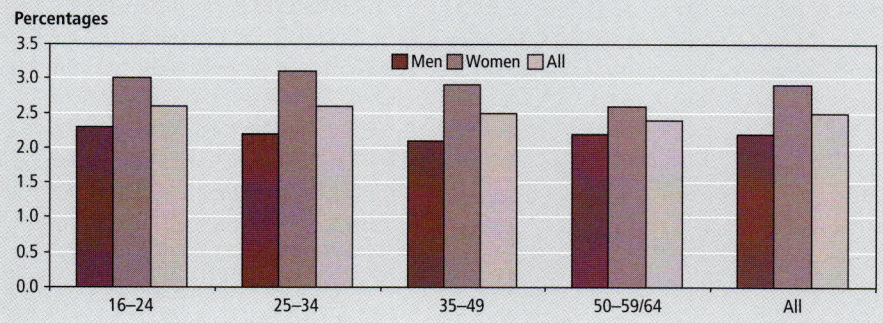

Percentages

Note: Source: Labour Force Survey

1   July to June for each period.

Figure 3
Sickness absence rates of working-age employees: by sex and age, July 2007 to June 2008

Percentages

Men Women All

Source: Labour Force Survey

per cent compared with 2.2 per cent for men. Analysis by age shows that younger employees are more likely to take sickness absence than older employees: 2.6 per cent of the 16 to 24 and 25 to 34 age groups were absent from work because of sickness or injury. This compares with 2.5 per cent for 35 to 49-year-olds and 2.4 per cent for employees aged 50 to 59/64. Among men, those aged 16 to 24 were the most likely to be absent due to sickness (2.3 per cent), whereas for women, those aged 25 to 34 had the highest rate of sickness absence (3.1 per cent).

Personal characteristics

Around 12.4 per cent of working-age employees classify themselves as disabled, of which 4.6 per cent were absent from work because of sickness or injury. In comparison, only 2.3 per cent of employees who do not classify themselves as disabled were absent from work.

Table 1 shows that the Black/Black British ethnic group has the highest sickness absence rates, at 3.8 per cent. The Asian/Asian British ethnic group has the lowest rates, at 2.3 per cent, while 2.5 per cent of those in the White ethnic

group were absent from work in the reference week.

Workplace characteristics

Table 1 shows that workplaces with fewer than 25 employees have a sickness absence rate of 2.3 per cent, compared with 2.8 per cent for those workplaces with over 500 employees. Recent findings published by the Chartered Institute of Personnel and Development stated that:

> smaller organisations typically record lower levels of absence because absence is more disruptive and harder to cover for. Smaller employers are also less likely to provide as generous occupational sick pay schemes as larger employers.

Sickness absence rates in the public sector remain the highest, at 2.9 per cent, compared with 2.4 per cent for those in the private sector. Using the LFS, sickness absence rates in the civil service are 3.5 per cent. As in the Cabinet Office sickness absence report, results from the LFS also show that women and part-timers working in the civil service are most likely to be absent from work due to sickness or injury.

Job tenure

Sickness absence varies by length of time in post. Those who have worked in the same workplace for more than five years but less than ten have a sickness absence rate of 2.7 per cent. For those who worked in the same workplace for less than three months, the sickness absence rate is 2.3 per cent. It is also 2.3 per cent for those working in the same workplace for more than 20 years.

Occupation

The LFS classifies occupation by nine major groups, using the 2000 Standard Occupational Classification. Sickness absence rates vary between occupations, from 2.0 per cent for 'managers and senior officials' to 3.1 per cent for 'personal service occupations' and 'administrative and secretarial occupations'. **Table 2** shows further analysis by detailed occupation breakdown. 'Customer service occupations' (for example, call centre agents/operators) have the highest sickness absence rates, at 4.8 per cent, while 'transport associate professionals' (for example, train drivers) have the lowest, at 0.8 per cent.

Working patterns

In the LFS, whether a respondent is working full-time is determined by their

Table 1

Sickness absence rates of working-age employees, July 2007 to June 2008

	Percentages
	Rate
Disability	
Disabled	4.6
Not disabled	2.3
Ethnicity	
White	2.5
Mixed	2.4
Asian or Asian British	2.3
Black or Black British	3.8
Chinese	2.4
Other	3.3
Workplace size	
Less than 25	2.3
25–49	2.7
50–499	2.6
500 or more	2.8
Total	2.5
Sector	
Public	2.9
Private	2.4
Job tenure	
Less than three months	2.3
Three months but less than six	2.4
Six months but less than 12	2.6
One year but less than two	2.6
Two years but less than five	2.6
Five years but less than ten	2.7
Ten years but less than 20	2.4
20 years or more	2.3
Occupation	
Managers and senior officials	2.0
Professional occupations	2.4
Associate professional and technical	2.4
Administrative and secretarial occupations	3.1
Skilled trades occupations	2.5
Personal service occupations	3.1
Sales and customer service occupations	2.8
Process, plant and machine operatives	2.7
Elementary occupations	2.4
Full-time/part-time	
Full-time	2.6
Part-time	2.4
Hours worked (including overtime)	
Less than 16	1.8
16–30	2.7
31–45	2.7
Over 45	2.1
Income	
Less than £300	2.9
£300-£399	3.0
£400-£499	3.0
£500-£599	2.4
£600+	2.2

Source: Labour Force Survey

own assessment and not the number of hours worked. Those working full-time have higher sickness absence rates than part-timers, 2.6 per cent compared with 2.4 per cent. Those working full-time are more likely to be absent from work on a Friday because of sickness or injury while part-timers are more likely to be absent on Wednesdays because of sickness or injury.

Analysis by hours worked (including overtime) shows that those working 16 to 30 hours or 31 to 45 hours per week have the highest sickness absence rates, at 2.7 per cent. In comparison, those working less than 16 hours have sickness absence rates of 1.8 per cent, while 2.1 per cent of those working over 45 hours per week were absent from work.

Sickness absence rates by income

Table 1 shows that sickness absence rates generally decrease as gross weekly pay increases. Those employees earning between £300 to £399 and £400 to £499 each week have sickness absence rates of 3.0 per cent while those earning more than £600 each week have rates of 2.2 per cent. This is consistent with research published by the Cabinet Office which found that those employees of higher grades in the public sector had fewer sick absences than those in lower grades (Cabinet Office 2007).

Statistical modelling of sickness absence

So far, this article has presented statistics for a variety of personal characteristics of those employees absent from work due to sickness or injury. A statistical technique known as logistic regression creates a model that considers a range of personal characteristics to determine which of these are most associated with employees having at least one day off in the reference week. Modelling looks at all the factors simultaneously to control for those that affect sickness absence rates.

The model introduces control variables for sex, occupation, disability, ethnicity, region, workplace size, sector, working pattern, hours worked, age band and job tenure. These are used to predict whether an individual has had a day off due to sickness or injury in the reference week. The analysis considers employees of working age in April to June 2008.

For each variable within the model, one category was selected as the reference category; this enables comparisons to be made with other categories within that variable. The reference category was usually that with the largest sample size.

Table 2
Sickness absence rates of working-age employees: by detailed occupation breakdown, July 2007 to June 2008

Percentages

	Rate
Five highest	
721 Customer service occupations	*4.8*
541 Textiles and garment trades	*4.3*
411 Administrative: government and related	*3.9*
342 Design associate professionals	*3.8*
912 Elementary construction occupations	*3.6*
Five lowest	
351 Transport associate professionals	*0.8*
241 Legal professionals	*1.0*
542 Printing trades	*1.1*
344 Sports and fitness occupations	*1.2*
117 Protective service officers	*1.3*

Source: Labour Force Survey

Figure 4 shows the impact of personal and labour market characteristics on the likelihood of the respondent being absent from work due to sickness or injury. The bars shaded magenta indicate where a category within a variable is estimated to be significantly different from the reference category at the 5 per cent significance level. As each estimate is drawn from a sample of the population, different samples could give different results. Statistical significance means that, at the 5 per cent significance level, it is 95 per cent certain that the estimated relationship is not due to chance. In the graph, only those variables where there is a significant relationship are shown.

The analysis shows that after controlling for other factors:

- women are 22 per cent more likely to be absent from work in the reference week than men
- those working in the public sector are 22 per cent more likely to be absent than those working in the private sector
- the Black/Black British ethnic group are 51 per cent more likely to be absent than the White ethnic group
- those working less than 16 hours per week are 47 per cent less likely to be absent than those working over 45 hours
- employees aged 16 to 24 are 32 per cent more likely to be absent than those aged 50 to 59/64
- those employees who classify themselves as disabled are almost 2.5 times more likely to be absent than those not disabled
- employees in 'personal service occupations' are 57 per cent more likely to be absent than those in the 'professional occupations'
- those in workplaces with more than 500 employees are 34 per cent more likely to be absent than those in workplaces with less than 25 employees

There were no significant differences in sickness absence patterns for grouped regions (London, South East, rest of England, Wales, Scotland and Northern Ireland), working pattern (full-time and part-time) or job tenure.

Notes

1 For more information on sickness absence rates, see www.statistics.gov.uk/statbase/product.asp?vlnk=14424

CONTACT

✉ elmr@ons.gsi.gov.uk

REFERENCES

Absence Management, Annual Survey Report 2008, Chartered Institute of Personnel and Development at www.cipd.co.uk/subjects/hrpract/absence/absmagmt.htm

Barham C and Leonard J (2002) 'Trends and sources of data on sickness absence', *Labour Market Trends* 110(4), pp 177–85.

Barham C and Begum N (2005) 'Sickness absence from work in the UK', *Labour Market Trends* 113(4), pp 149–58.

Cabinet Office (2007) 'Civil Service sickness absence 2006–2007' at www.civilservice.gov.uk/about/statistics/sickness.asp

Machin A and Millard B (2007) 'Characteristics of public sector workers', *Economic & Labour Market Review* 1(5), pp 46–55 and at www.statistics.gov.uk/cci/article.asp?id=1801

Sickies and Long-Term Absence give employers a headache – CBI/AXA Survey (May 2008) at www.cbi.org.uk/ndbs/press.nsf/0363c1f07c6ca12a8025671c00381cc7/90ab71d2f4d981da8025744200523b87?OpenDocument

Figure 4
Impact of various characteristics on the odds of a respondent being absent due to sickness or injury in the reference week

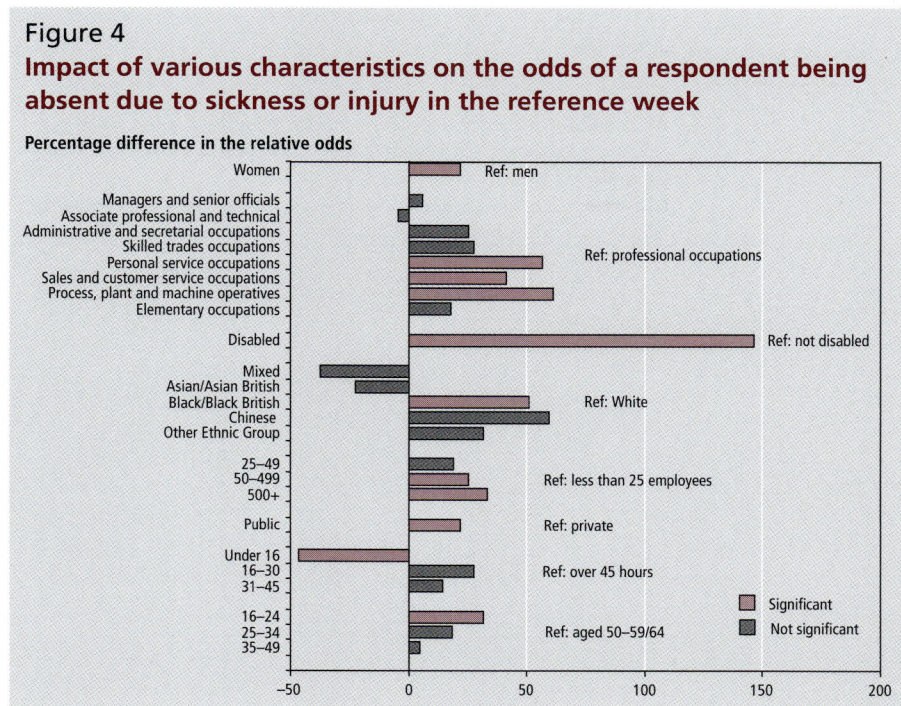

Source: Labour Force Survey

APPENDIX

Table A1
Other sources of sickness absence data

Source	Key findings
Confederation of British Industry Absence and labour turnover, May 2008	Analysis based on replies from 503 companies who together employ more than 1 million employees, equivalent to 3.6 per cent of the UK workforce. In 2007, direct cost of absence £13.2 billion or £517 each employee. Indirect costs add another £263 per employee. Total cost of absence comes to £19.9 billion. Average employee took 6.7 days off sick. 172 million days lost to sickness absence, 12 per cent thought to be non-genuine. 5 per cent of absence spells became long-term (20 days or more), accounting for 40 per cent of all time lost. Average absence levels in the public sector stood at 9 days compared with 5.8 days in the private sector. Organisations that recognised trade unions saw three days' more absence than in non-unionised workplaces. Strong regional differences across the UK. North West and Yorkshire and The Humber lost most days, Southern England the least. Minor ailments, such as colds, are the most significant cause of short-term absence; back pain came second.
Chartered Institute of Personnel and Development Absence measurement and management, July 2008	Analysis based on replies from 819 UK-based HR professionals in organisations employing more than 2.3 million employees. The average sickness absence was 3.5 per cent, or 8.0 working days each employee. The average annual cost of absence each employee was estimated at £666. Absence levels in the public sector remain the highest. Only 40 per cent of respondent organisations monitor the cost of absence. The main cause of short-term absence for both manual and non-manual workers is minor illness such as colds, flu and stomach upsets. Smaller organisations typically record lower levels of absence because absence is more disruptive and harder to cover for. The main causes of long-term absence (four weeks or more) among manual workers are acute medical conditions, followed by back pain, musculoskeletal conditions, stress and mental health problems.
Cabinet Office Analysis of sickness absence in the civil service, February 2008	Almost 50 per cent of civil servants had no recorded absence in 2006/07 and over three-quarters of the civil service took fewer than five working days off sick. Total cost of absence was estimated at £393million. Average working days lost each staff year is 9.63. Younger staff have more spells of absence, but these are shorter than for older staff. Women have more spells of absence than men. Staff in the lower grades have a tendency to take more spells and longer spells than those at higher grades. Mental disorders and musculoskeletal accounted for around a third (34 per cent) of all days lost. For all lengths of absence, there is a trend for spells to end so return to work will be on a Monday. For shorter-term absences, there is a trend for spells to start at the beginning of the week. Shift workers tended to have proportionally more spells and for these to be longer than for full-time workers. For part-time workers, this pattern was even more pronounced.

Economic & Labour Market Review | Vol 2 | No 11 | November 2008

FEATURE

Peter Goodridge
Office for National Statistics

Analysis of international trade and productivity, using the EUKLEMS database

SUMMARY

This article presents analysis on the possible impact of international trade on industrial productivity in the UK using the new EUKLEMS analytical database, in conjunction with Office for National Statistics Input-Output Supply Use tables. The aim is to also illustrate the breadth of opportunities the database offers potential users for a wide variety of economic research.

The KLEMS project, funded by the European Union and coordinated by the University of Groningen and the National Institute of Economic and Social Research, was a three-year project initiated with the objective of creating an internationally comparable database of measures relating to economic growth, employment, productivity, capital formation and technological change, for all member states. A handful of other competing economies were also included for comparison, primarily the US, Japan, Korea and Canada. Particular attention has been paid to producing data suitable for growth accounting analysis, with the name of the project being derived from the factor and intermediate inputs to production (capital, labour, energy, materials and services). The inclusion of energy, materials and services means that growth-accounting techniques can be used to estimate the contributions of intermediate inputs to output growth, in addition to those of capital and labour in more traditional analysis, resulting in a finer assessment of multi-factor productivity (MFP) growth, that is, output growth not attributable to the factors and intermediate inputs to production. The database[1] was released in March 2008.

The next phase of the project is to transfer the management and population of the database to Eurostat and the National Statistical Institutes, creating the 'statistical' database, which should be constructed with more statistically rigorous data. This second phase is at its inception now, and is expected to become live by late-2009 or 2010.

The analysis in this article uses KLEMS output, employment and productivity data alongside industrial trade data from the Input-Output (I-O) Supply Use tables to assess theories on the impact of international trade on domestic productivity, including those put forward by Balassa and Samuelson and the original theories of Adam Smith and David Ricardo.

However, the database also contains a vast amount of data on labour input (including labour composition or 'quality'), capital services and intermediate inputs at a detailed industrial level, which could be used for a wide range of productivity and economic analyses. One of the main advantages of the database is that common methodologies have been applied across data from different member states, based on the System of National Accounts (SNA93), allowing meaningful international comparisons to be made and allowing research to be replicated for different countries (or groups of countries).

Theory

The acceptance of the mutual benefits acquired through free trade in terms of improved productivity and increased living standards goes all the way back to Adam Smith and, later, David Ricardo. More recently, similar arguments have been put forward by Balassa and Samuelson who, in other work on relative prices and exchange rates, argued that the most productive industries are those exposed to greater competition from international markets. By having to compete on an international basis, in both domestic and foreign markets, firms are forced to improve efficiency and price more competitively, compared with those that operate in industries relatively closed to international trade.

The Balassa-Samuelson hypothesis states that, where output can be internationally traded, prices will conform to a 'world price' and countries with a productivity advantage will specialise in that industry and supply the world market. Therefore, it is reasonable to expect a firm or industry that produces exports to experience higher productivity relative to more closed sectors. In contrast, firms or industries producing non-tradeable products will not face the same intensity of competition, since the transaction naturally takes place at a more local level. In general, more cases of non-tradeable output are found in the service sector, with an obvious example being a haircut. An illustration of the effect can be seen in the differential between alcohol prices in pubs and supermarkets – the former is a local transaction with limited competition while the latter is subject to much greater competition due to transport and distribution networks.

It is also intuitive that international exposure will force firms to increase productivity in a number of ways. As well as competing with domestic firms, they will also have to compete with the most productive firms from other markets. This will, among other things, encourage them to improve the quality of their labour, invest in greater quantities and qualities of capital, improve their management and organisational structure, improve the efficiency of their business processes and adopt best international practice. In turn, this will serve to reduce costs in order to remain competitive, and as a result improve productivity. Indeed, competition has been identified by HM Treasury and the Department for Business, Enterprise & Regulatory Reform as a key driver of productivity growth, as have investment, innovation, skills and enterprise.

As mentioned above, the benefits of international trade to domestic productivity have been recognised since Adam Smith proposed his theory of 'Absolute Advantage', stating that a country should specialise in, and export, products in which it is most productive, and import those goods which the country can produce less efficiently (Smith 1776). Therefore, the country will gain by purchasing some goods for less than they would have cost to produce domestically, and selling more of what it can produce more efficiently abroad. As

a result, the value of consumption and production will increase, resulting in higher national income and living standards, and international market forces will help allocate capital and labour to industries where the productive advantage lies.

Ricardo built on Smith's model, stating that there will be mutual gains from trade even if one country does not have an absolute advantage in any particular industry, provided it specialises where it has the greatest comparative advantage (or, put another way, least absolute disadvantage). The immediate implication of Smith and Ricardo's work is that countries will specialise in industries where they have a natural productivity advantage, and hence productivity will be higher in the more trade-intensive and export-intensive sectors.

Although Ricardo improved on Smith's theory by introducing the element of relative productivity, his model was quite static. However, Smith's work had other, more dynamic, implications for productivity. International trade serves to increase the size of the potential market which, Smith argued, provides the only limit to the division (or specialisation) of labour. He argued that specialisation increases productivity by improving the skill level, and competence, of labour, saving time and facilitating invention and innovation, with the latter being the key to increased productivity and economic growth. This creates a virtuous circle where increased trade leads to increased consumption and investment, greater enterprise, increased capital formation, further division of labour, increased productivity and more trade.

Therefore, in more modern terms, Smith proposed that trade would help increase productivity by allowing firms to benefit from increasing returns to (and economies of) scale by increasing the size of the market, which would allow increased division of labour, thereby improving the efficiency of business

processes and facilitating technological change by providing greater returns to capital investment. So, according to Smith, international trade promotes what are now considered the key drivers of productivity growth – skills, investment, innovation, competition and enterprise.

Data source
All data used have been taken from the EUKLEMS database and supplemented with trade figures from the I-O Supply Use tables in the National Accounts. To allow comparisons over time, all current price data have been deflated to remove price effects. Also, all analysis refers to 1992 to 2004, using the full period for which I-O tables are available, to reduce volatility and eliminate cyclical effects as far as possible. **Table 1** lists all variables used and their source.

Analysis
The following analysis will assess whether industrial-level data support the theories outlined above in terms of the associations between trade intensity, export intensity, labour productivity and the contribution of multi-factor productivity. The data are presented mainly at two-digit industry level, according to the Standard Industrial Classification (SIC), and split into 30 separate industries. A description and list of the industries is provided in **Table A1** in the Appendix.

To help identify industries where trade is most significant, **Figure 1** plots the trade intensity ranking of each industry between 1992 and 2004. The measure used for trade intensity is simply the sum of exports and imports expressed as a ratio to gross output, for that particular industry.

As can be seen, the rankings are fairly stable across years and the most trade-intensive industries are consistently located in the manufacturing sector, in particular Office and computing machinery, communication and medical equipment; Textiles, leather and footwear; Motor

Table 1
Input data

Source	Series name	Description
EUKLEMS database	VA	Gross value added at current basic prices (£ million)
	H_EMP	Total hours worked by persons engaged (millions)
	GO	Gross output at current basic prices (£ million)
	GO_P	Gross output, price indices, 1995=100
	LP_I	Gross value added per hour worked, volume indices, 1995=100
	GOConTFP	Contribution of total factor productivity (TFP) to output growth (percentage points)
	TFPgo_I	TFP (gross output based) growth, 1995=100
	GO_QI	Gross output, volume indices, 1995=100
I-O supply use	Total exports of goods and services	Total exports by product/industry (£ million)
	Total imports of goods and services	Total imports by product/industry (£ million)

vehicles and other transport equipment; Chemicals; Coke, petroleum and nuclear fuel; and Machinery. Also within production, fairly high levels of trade intensity exist in Mining and quarrying. In the service sector, the highest ranking industries are Transport, Business services, Financial intermediation and, perhaps surprisingly, Hotels and restaurants. However, these services are ranked between 15 and 20 out of all 30 industry groups, compared with manufacturing, where the average ranking is approximately 8.

Figure 2 is presented in the same format, only this time ranking the labour productivity (real gross value added (GVA) per hour) performance of each industry over the same period.

Closer inspection of the graphs shows that there does appear to be some correlation between the most trade intensive and the most productive industries, but there are a number of exceptions. The most notable are Real estate and Utilities, where the high productivity levels are a reflection of the high property and energy prices, and industry profits, seen in recent years, generating very high levels of GVA. In the case of Utilities, the situation is exacerbated by the creation of private monopolies at around the start of the period studies. Also, due to their domestic nature, the scope for any impact of trade in either industry is limited. High prices and profits, as well as the industries' capital-intensive nature, have also affected GVA in Mining and quarrying, although there is also a significant volume of trade in this industry.

After taking account of these anomalies, in general, the most productive industries tend to be in manufacturing, in particular

Figure 1
Trade intensity rankings: by two-digit SIC group

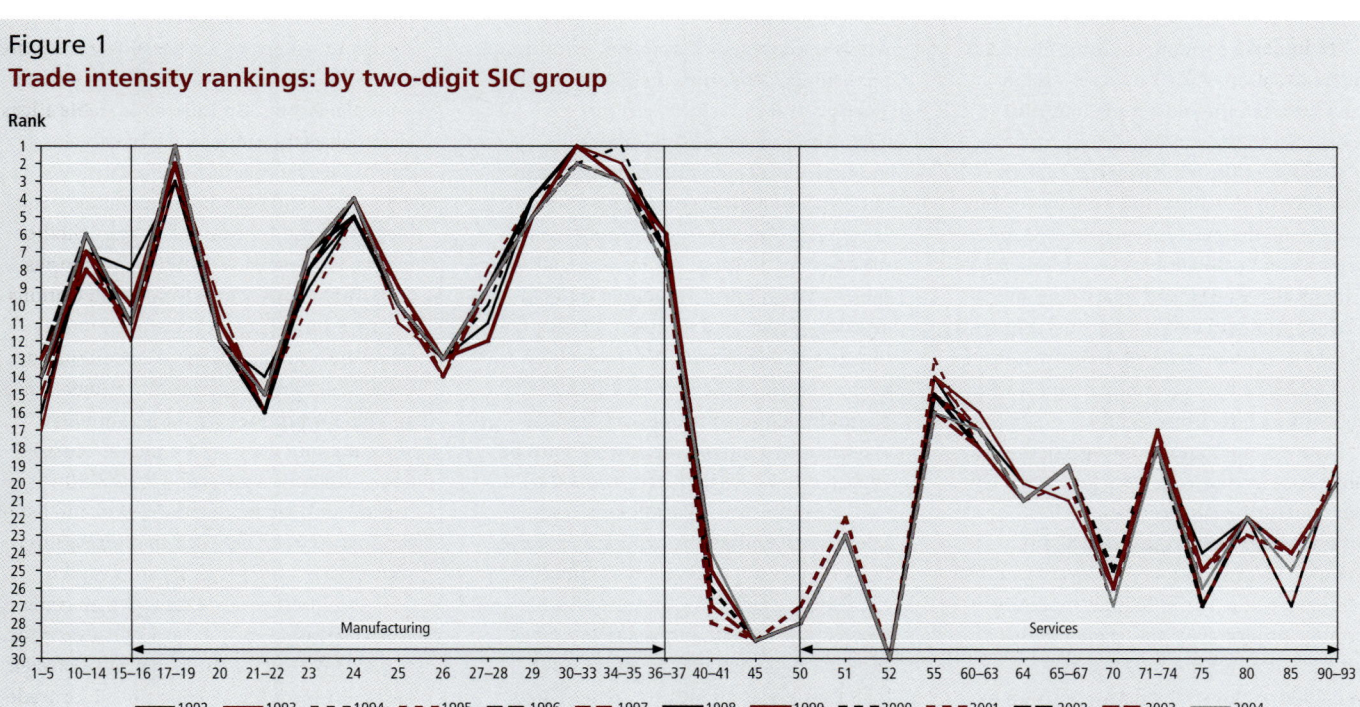

Figure 2
Labour productivity rankings: by two-digit SIC group

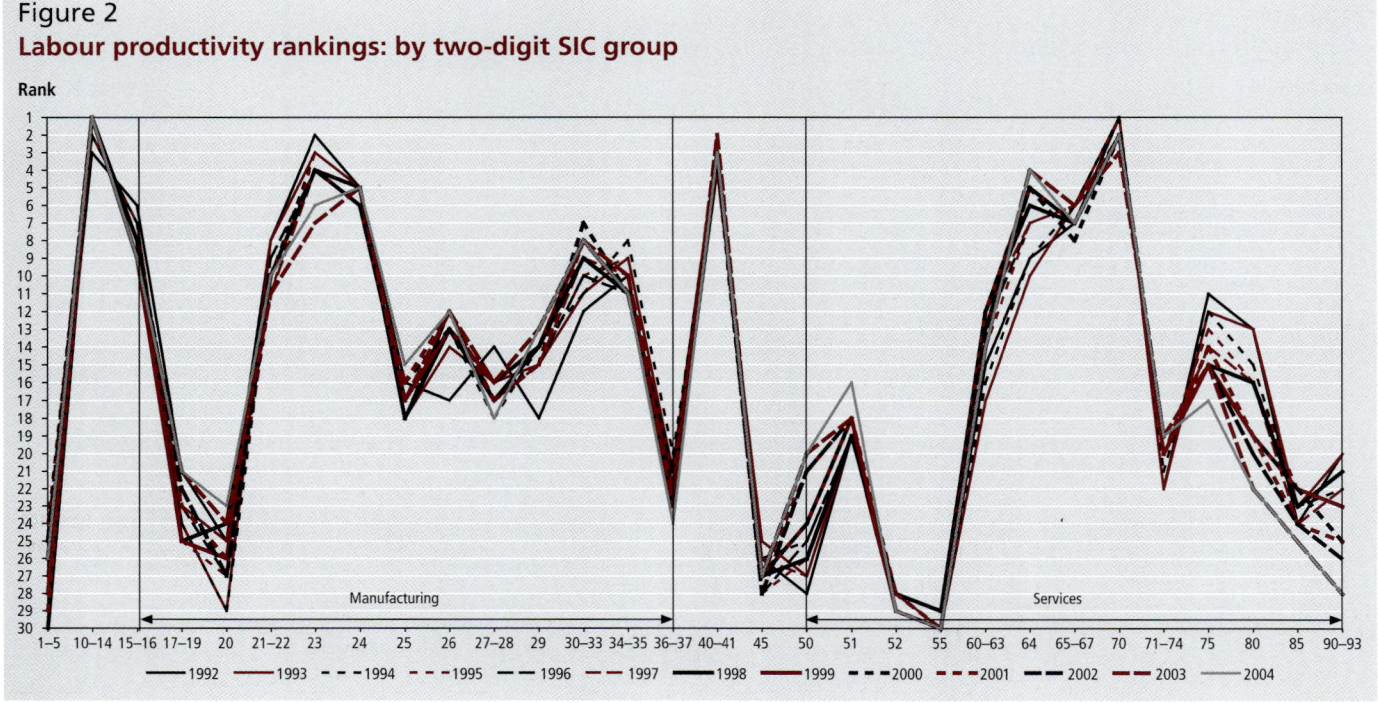

Coke, petroleum and nuclear fuel; Chemicals; Food, beverages and tobacco; Office and computing machinery, communication and medical equipment; and Motor vehicles and other transport equipment, with most of these industries having high levels of trade intensity, particularly Chemicals; Office and computing machinery, communication and medical equipment; and Motor vehicles and other transport equipment. Again, recent trends in energy-related industries will have had some effect in the case of Coke, petroleum and nuclear fuel.

In terms of services (leaving aside Real estate), the more productive industries – Post and telecommunications, Financial intermediation, and Transport – again largely match the most trade intensive industries in the service sector.

Overall, of the ten industries that are consistently the most trade-intensive, four are among the most productive – Motor vehicles and other transport equipment; Chemicals; Mining and quarrying; and Coke, petroleum and nuclear fuel. **Figure 3** plots the average trade intensity by industry alongside the average productivity level to show this a little more clearly.

Figure 3 illustrates more starkly the difference in trade intensity between manufacturing and services, with an average industry value of 0.82 in manufacturing, compared with 0.11 in the services sector. The bold lines represent average productivity and trade intensity for the whole economy between 1992 and 2004 to show the relative position of

each industry. Almost all of the industries in manufacturing are above the whole economy measures for both trade intensity and productivity, while the opposite is true for most industries in the service sector. There also appears to be a correlation between average trade and productivity levels in industries previously mentioned, such as Mining and quarrying; Chemicals; and Coke, petroleum and nuclear fuel, which all experience relatively high levels of both trade intensity and labour productivity. There are also a number of industries, where trade is at a similar level to the whole economy average, which experience similar productivity levels to the whole economy, such as Paper, printing and publishing; Other non-metallic minerals; Transport; and Business services.

However, there are a number of industries which do not conform to this pattern, although in some cases there are a number of industry-specific issues which may be contributing. For instance, although there is a significant volume of trade in Textiles, leather and footwear, the amount that consists of imports has grown due to the decline of the domestic industry. Naturally, a domestic industry that has experienced a fall in output would not be expected to be particularly productive. One industry that is particularly trade-intensive that might be expected to show higher levels of productivity is Office and computing machinery, communication and medical equipment, but again a number of industry factors may be preventing this. Firstly, it is an industry where there

are inherent issues in the measurement of quality and therefore price and output. Secondly, international competition may be squeezing margins in an industry where there is a very clearly defined value chain. This also applies to other technology industries such as Machinery. Thirdly, there may be an under-recording of some of the investment that takes place in the industry (for example, software investment). Other industries with characteristics that inhibit any relationship, such as Mining and quarrying, Real estate and Utilities have already been discussed.

Although the relationship is far from clear cut, it should be borne in mind that Figure 3 includes industries where trade is limited by the nature of the industry (for example, Public administration, Education, Health), where productivity may be lower due to the fact that most activity is outside the market and output is often inadequately measured and based on the volume of inputs. However, even after removing these and other almost entirely domestically-oriented industries (for example, Real estate and Construction), a correlation coefficient between series for trade intensity and labour productivity levels shows an association of only +0.1, which is certainly not statistically significant.

It should also be noted that any productivity gap between manufacturing and services should not be attributed to differing levels of trade intensity. In general, services tend to exhibit lower productivity, commonly referred to as 'Baumol's Disease' or the 'Baumol Effect' (Baumol and Bowen

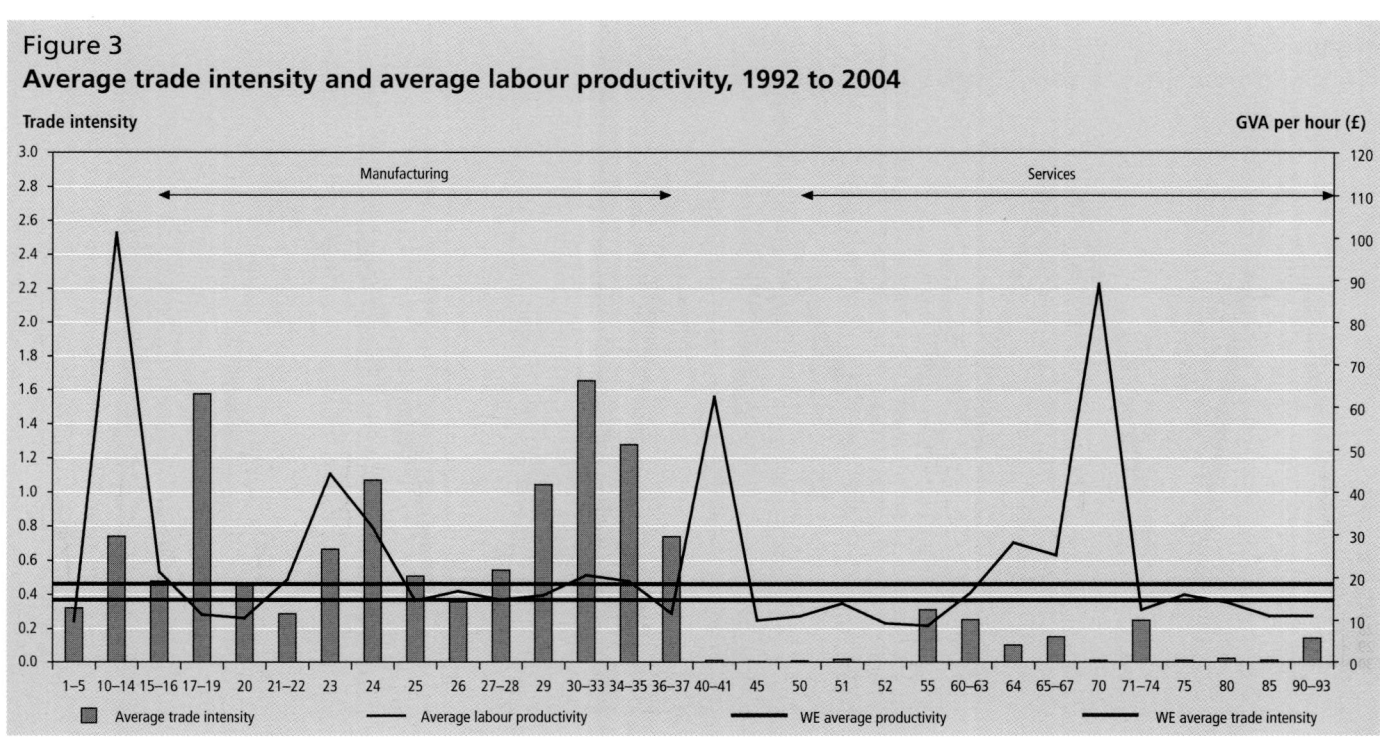

Figure 3
Average trade intensity and average labour productivity, 1992 to 2004

1966). This is a reflection of services generally being more labour intensive than production industries and therefore benefiting less from technological advance. Rather than a means to production, the product of labour is often the service itself, with Baumol's example being that it takes the same number of musicians to play a Beethoven string quartet today as it did in the 19th century. This applies to various service sector industries; for instance, it is hard to conceive of how productivity improvements among hairdressers could be as significant as those among manufacturers, where capital intensity and the scope for automation are far greater. It is also difficult for service delivery, which often includes a tailored or personalised service, to benefit from the division of labour in the same way as a production/assembly line might in a manufacturing firm.

However, for some service sector industries, this lack of ability to benefit from capital formation and technical progress appears to be changing with developments in information and communication technology (ICT) resulting in considerable product and process innovation, particularly in finance and business services (OECD 2007). Linking back to Baumol's observations, the output of a string quartet increases exponentially if the performance is either broadcast or recorded and distributed. It should also be borne in mind that improvements in the quality of service sector output are often not adequately captured in

official data, meaning productivity in this sector is actually understated. Although frequently mentioned when discussing services provided by the public sector, it is sometimes forgotten that this issue also applies to many private sector services. The problem is particularly acute in financial services, although it is envisaged that measurement of output in this sector will improve with the new methodology for financial intermediation services indirectly measured, introduced in the National Accounts in *Blue Book 2008*. Another possible factor may be that as the UK economy, and therefore labour, is constantly shifting away from manufacturing, the remaining labour force being drawn into services is less productive, causing any inherent productivity gap to widen slightly.

Therefore, there does appear to be some evidence to support the theory that trade and greater market exposure encourages gains in productivity due to more intense competitive pressures. However, the evidence is relatively limited, even though at the aggregate sector level – manufacturing versus services – the evidence is a bit more convincing.

The following analysis, illustrated in **Figure 4**, takes a closer look at export intensity in the context of the theories proposed by Smith and Ricardo.

Figure 4 again illustrates the stark contrast between manufacturing and services, this time in the context of export intensity. However, there is also considerable variation within manufacturing. The following industries

are among the most export intensive: Office and computing machinery, communication and medical equipment; Chemicals; Motor vehicles and other transport equipment; Machinery; Textiles, leather and footwear; and Mining and quarrying. In services, the most prominent exporters are Business services, Financial intermediation and Transport. The former two are not surprising given the resources allocated to these industries in the last decade or so.

Again, there is some correlation between the most export-intensive and most productive industries, especially in the cases of Chemicals, Mining, Financial intermediation, Transport, and Office and computing machinery, but perhaps not as much as might be expected. To illustrate the relationship, or lack of one, **Figure 5** plots average export intensity against average GVA per hour.

As can be seen, the evidence is mixed. For instance, industries such as Agriculture and fishing, Wood and cork, Wholesale, and Other services conform to the theory in that they have a lower level of export intensity than the whole economy, and a lower level of labour productivity. Additionally, industries such as Mining and quarrying; Coke, petroleum and nuclear fuel; and Chemicals have relatively high levels of export intensity and experience high labour productivity. Others, including Food, beverages and tobacco; Other non-metallic minerals; Transport; and Business services have a similar level of export intensity to the whole economy and a similar level of labour productivity to the

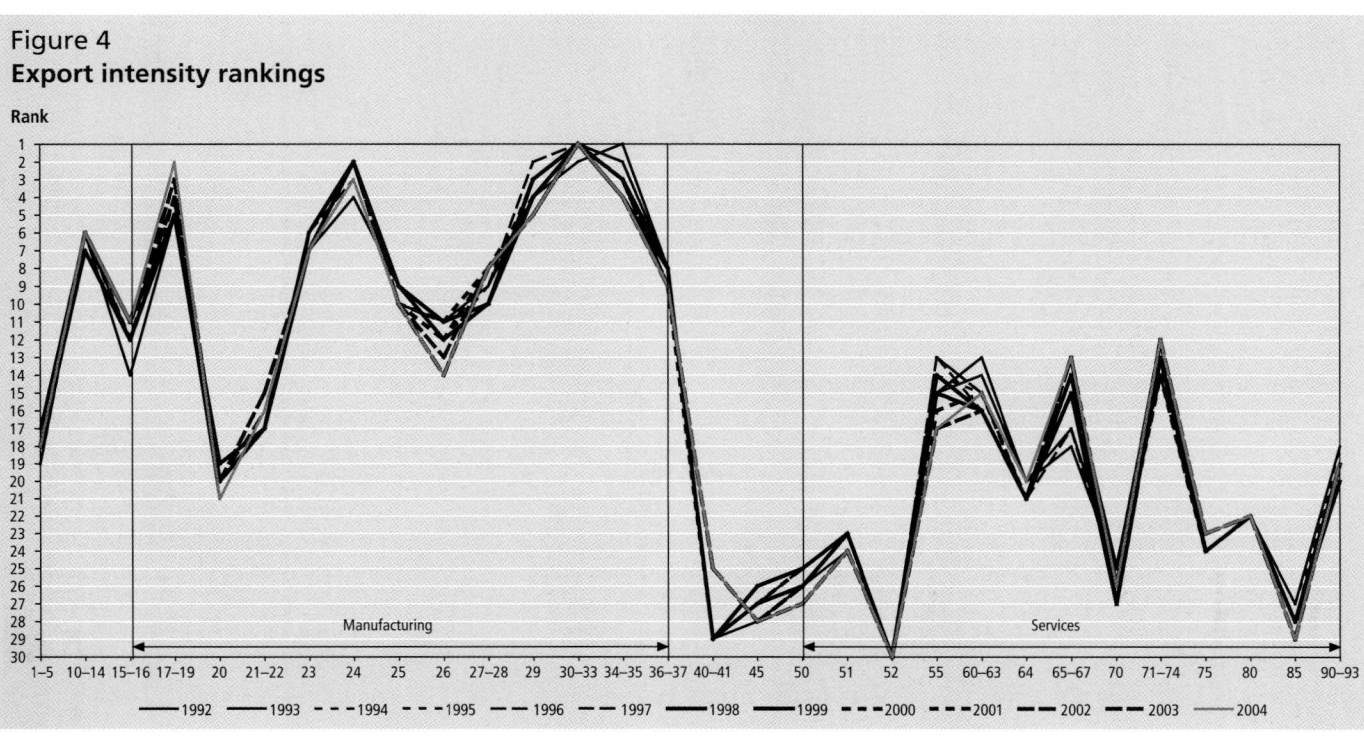

Figure 4
Export intensity rankings

Figure 5
Average export intensity and average labour productivity, 1992 to 2004

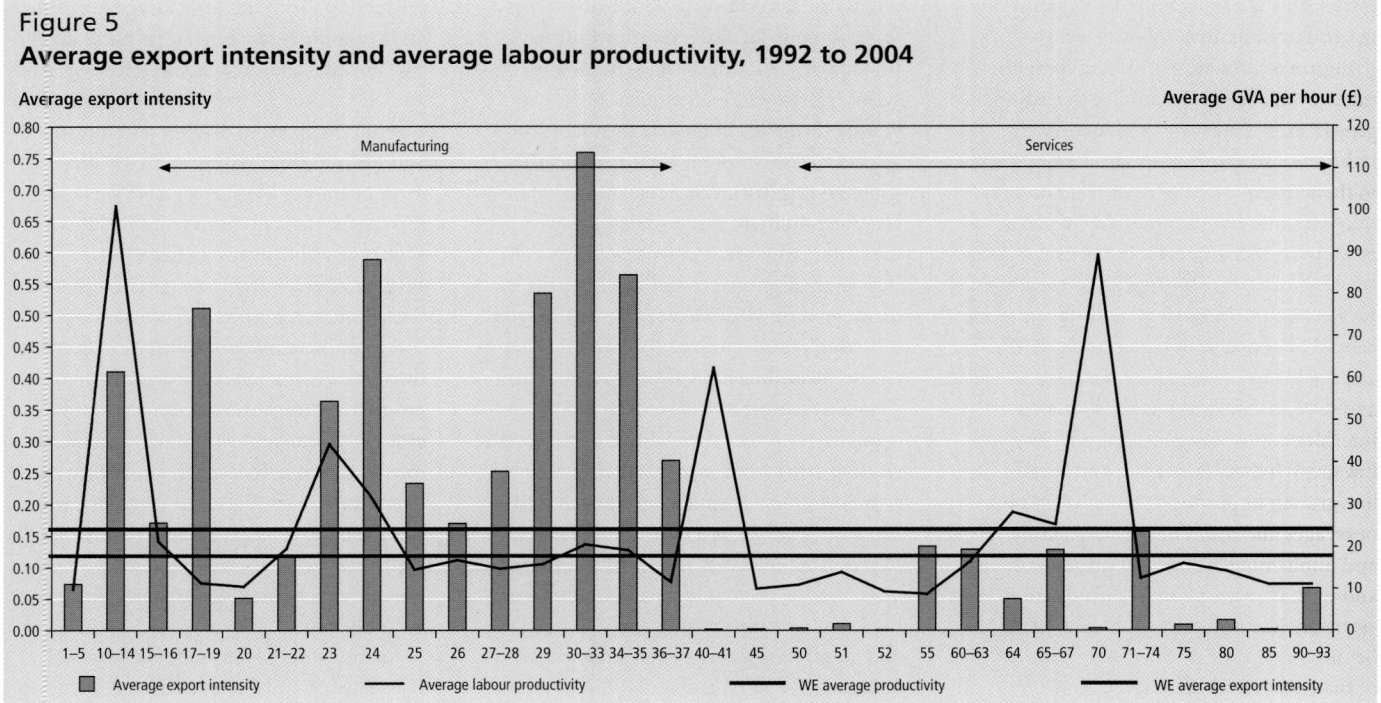

Figure 6
Trade intensity and labour productivity, average annual growth, 1992 to 2004

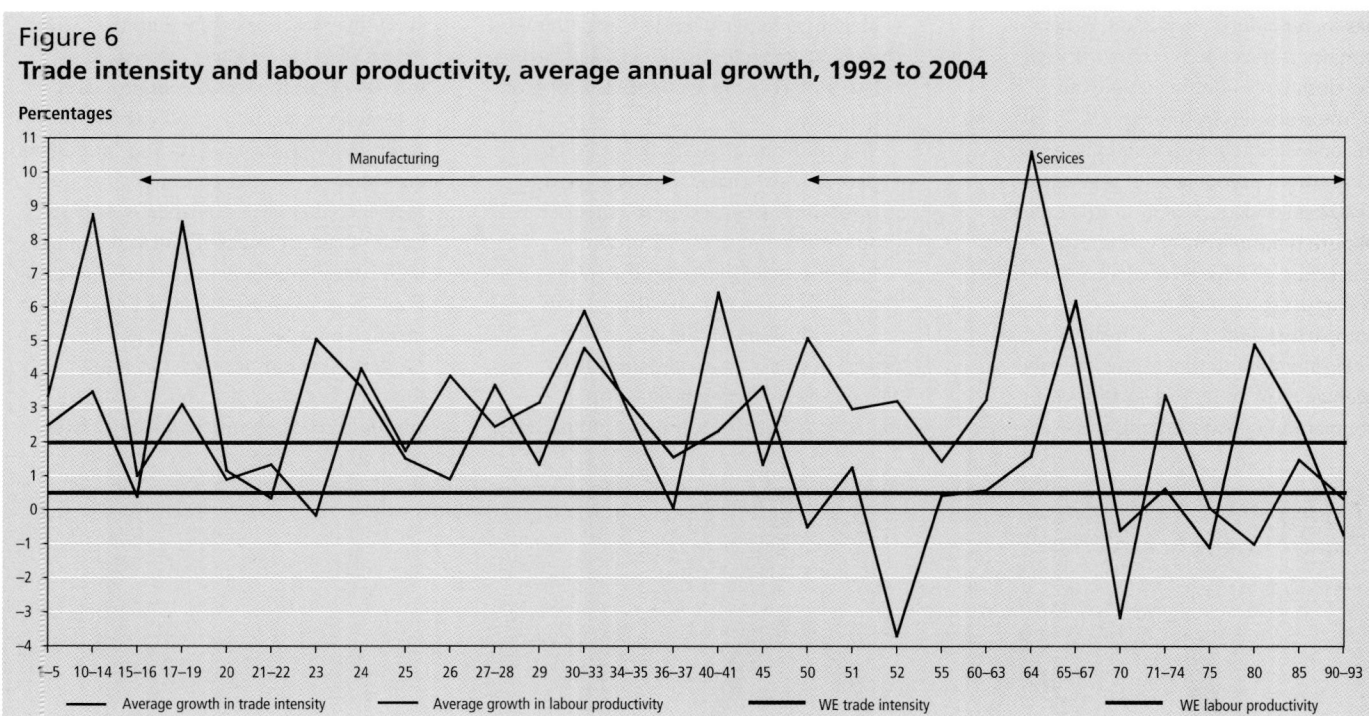

whole economy. However, there are also several industries that do not conform to this pattern, for example, Textiles, leather and footwear; Machinery; Office and computing machinery, communication and medical equipment; and Motor vehicles and other transport equipment have low levels of labour productivity than would not be expected given their relatively high levels of export intensity. In the case of Textiles, leather and footwear, there have been changes to the structure of the industry while both measurement and industry-specific factors may play a role

in the technology industries, as explained previously.

In terms of correlation, after removing industries where the nature of the market means it is not really appropriate to consider export volumes, the correlation coefficient between the two measures is +0.25, again positive, but not strong.

Again, the data do not appear to show a strong link between export intensity and labour productivity levels, though there are reasons for some of the exceptions.

However, in some respects, this is not unreasonable. It does not necessarily

always follow that an industry with a high level of trade intensity should generate high levels of value added per unit of labour, and it is possible that a sector can generate high levels of value added but not be conducive to trade (for example, Real estate). Alternatively, the added competition resulting from trade may squeeze margins to the extent that value added is relatively low, and current technology does not allow for further productivity improvements. In terms of the impact that trade will have, it seems possible that any correlation between trade intensity and productivity will exist more in growth rates rather than levels.

Figure 6 plots average annual growth rates of trade intensity alongside average growth rates in labour productivity, by industry, and shows their position relative to the whole economy. For the majority of industries, approximately two-thirds, high growth in trade intensity is associated with strong growth in labour productivity, and vice versa. The clearest cases of this include Mining and quarrying; Chemicals; Office and computing machinery; Utilities; Post and telecommunications; and Financial intermediation. Cases where relatively low growth in trade is associated with low growth in productivity include Food, beverages and tobacco; Paper, printing and publishing; Hotels and restaurants; and Other services. (As noted earlier, Real estate and public sector activities should be discounted in this context). In the cases of the energy and telecommunication markets, growth in trade and productivity has increased due to the structural change that has taken place in terms of both privatisation and the opening of markets.

The main exceptions to the pattern include Coke, petroleum and nuclear fuel; Construction; Motor vehicle distribution; and Retail trade. Therefore, although the picture is fairly mixed, in the majority of cases the expected association holds true, and appears slightly stronger than when comparing levels.

Figure 7 is similar to Figure 6, except that average growth rates in export intensity are compared with labour productivity growth.

This time, the pattern is slightly less obvious but, again, in the majority of cases, there is an association between export-intensive and more productive sectors and vice versa. After discounting industries where trade is naturally almost entirely domestically-oriented, the association becomes a little stronger. Also, although trade may be more limited in certain industries, it is still possible that productivity is higher as a result of international 'openness' in the form of international firms physically entering the domestic market. The obvious example here would be in Retail trade which, despite the increase in sales over the internet (often in domestic firms), is still relatively closed to international competition compared with the service sector as a whole. However, the entry of successful productive firms from abroad into the domestic market can help achieve the same result.

Obviously, most of the trade-intensive industries are also the most export-intensive and so any link is found mainly in the industries mentioned above in relation to growth in overall trade. There are some differences, though, including Food, beverages and tobacco and Paper, printing and publishing, which have experienced relatively high growth in export intensity and relatively low growth in labour productivity.

Returning to Adam Smith's hypotheses discussed earlier, perhaps the most dynamic and insightful aspect was the idea that large increases in the extent of the potential market made it more profitable to invent and innovate, thus increasing productivity.

Bearing this in mind, it seems reasonable that industries experiencing high growth in export intensity will have both the incentive and ability to benefit from technological change to a greater extent.

In growth-accounting analyses, output growth is assigned to growth in inputs, with the residual referred to as MFP, which is considered to be an approximation of disembodied technical change (examples could include increased knowledge and improved technology as a result of R&D, or improved management/organisational structures). In general, it captures any growth in output not explained by growth in inputs. Embodied technical change, in the form of capital improvements, will already be captured in the investment/capital data.

Table 2 compares growth of export intensity with MFP growth to see if there is any correlation between the two, to test the theory that increased access to international markets provides firms with the incentive (in the form of economies of scale) to develop and benefit from new technologies and improved business processes, thus increasing MFP growth in that industry.

As can be seen, it does seem that MFP growth makes its biggest contribution to output growth in industries most engaged in international markets and growing in terms of export intensity, with the most notable cases including those previously mentioned in terms of their level of trade intensity and productivity performance (that is, Mining, Chemicals, Office and computing machinery. Other industries

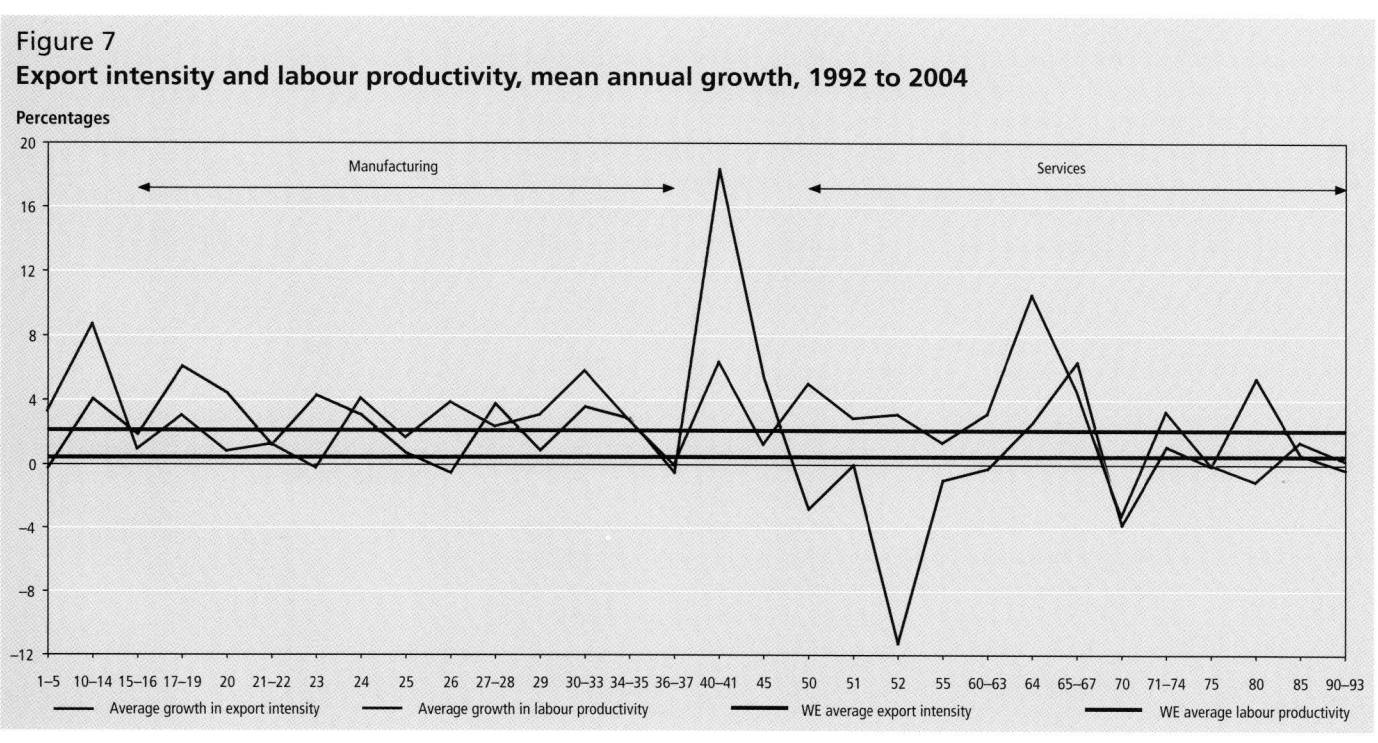

Figure 7
Export intensity and labour productivity, mean annual growth, 1992 to 2004

Table 2
MFP growth and export intensity

Percentages, except where indicated

SIC	MFP growth (mean)	Percentage point contribution of MFP to output growth (mean)	Output growth (mean)	MFP growth as a percentage of output growth (mean)	Growth in export intensity (mean)
1–5	1.06	1.01	–0.73		–0.24
10–14	1.65	1.54	0.45	341.72	4.06
15–16	–0.07	–0.08	0.72		1.88
17–19	0.42	0.40	–3.77		6.08
20	–0.28	–0.29	1.10		4.43
21–22	0.01	0.01	1.31	0.52	1.24
23	–0.20	–0.20	1.61		4.29
24	0.91	0.90	2.45	36.64	3.09
25	0.31	0.29	2.39	12.31	0.73
26	1.02	1.00	1.47	67.70	–0.52
27–28	0.50	0.50	–0.04		3.77
29	0.57	0.56	0.65	85.62	0.90
30–33	1.31	1.28	3.19	40.21	3.59
34–35	0.50	0.49	2.98	16.58	2.87
36–37	–0.58	–0.60	3.47		–0.49
40–41	0.48	0.47	1.86	25.31	18.38
45	0.31	0.30	2.62	11.54	5.39
50	1.12	1.09	4.64	23.57	–2.79
51	0.86	0.84	4.23	19.86	–0.01
52	0.60	0.58	4.84	11.94	–11.26
55	–0.17	–0.17	6.13		–0.97
60–63	0.79	0.78	4.94	15.76	–0.24
64	3.91	3.79	9.59	39.53	2.61
65–67	0.80	0.78	4.11	19.04	6.35
70	–1.16	–1.19	2.72		–3.80
71–74	0.13	0.11	7.07	1.61	1.14
75	–0.57	–0.58	1.93		–0.09
80	–1.02	–1.06	2.78		5.34
85	0.26	0.26	4.51	5.72	0.64
90–93	–0.64	–0.66	4.00		–0.30

Note:

Positive association in white; negative association shaded grey.

with relatively strong growth in both export intensity and MFP include Textiles, leather and footwear; Basic and fabricated metals; and Post and telecommunications. Additionally, many of the sectors with low or negative MFP growth are those not experiencing increased growth in export intensity – the clearest examples of this are Paper, printing and publishing; Rubber and plastics; and Manufacturing not elsewhere classified. The expected positive association holds in two-thirds of industries considered.

However, again, there are a number of exceptions. For instance, Food, beverages and tobacco; Wood and cork; and Coke, petroleum and nuclear fuel have all experienced strong growth in export intensity but negative growth in MFP.

It is likely that any effect here is transmitted in various ways. As well as the competitive element and profit incentive already discussed, industries and markets that are more internationally open are also more likely to achieve MFP growth as a result of firms building international networks in areas of mutual interest, increased collaboration and the diffusion of best practice, as well as via increased activity of multinational firms.

Conclusions

This article has examined the relationship between trade/export intensity and productivity growth – both labour and MFP. While there is some evidence to support the relevant theories (Balassa-Samuelson, Smith and Ricardo), the evidence is not overwhelming – some industries exhibit the relationship, but others do not. In broad terms, there does seem to be some correlation especially in terms of the difference between manufacturing and services, but at a more detailed industry level, the evidence is more mixed. For some sectors, consumption and production are both almost entirely domestic, for example, public sector services, construction and distribution. If these sectors are removed from the analysis, the correlation between trade or export intensity and productivity is stronger.

It should be noted that any relationship between trade and productivity should be thought of as circular, and causation should not be implied – the positive effects of trade will improve the productivity of the domestic industry, which will improve prospects for trade, increasing the potential for further profits, investment and productivity growth in a virtuous circle, as Smith argued in his original theories. It should be noted, though, that the increase in the size of the market may simply allow a small number of firms to overcome high barriers to entry and the market may not necessarily be competitive.

However, in general, trade improves the competitive environment, encouraging enterprise and innovation by increasing opportunities for, and potential returns to, investment, improving the possibilities to achieve economies of scale, encouraging the adoption of best practice and more. This seems increasingly relevant in light of recent trade negotiations and the continued presence of protectionist policies and highlights that, although useful, the Solow growth model and traditional growth analyses tend to neglect the possible contribution of trade to growth in productivity and living standards.

Notes

1   For further information, see www.euklems.net

CONTACT

 elmr@ons.gsi.gov.uk

REFERENCES

Baumol W J and Bowen W G (1966) 'Performing Arts: The Economic Dilemma', New York: The Twentieth Century Fund.

OECD (2007) 'Summary Report of the Study on Globalisation and Innovation in the Business Services Sector' at www.oecd.org/dataoecd/18/55/38619867.pdf

ONS (2007), *The ONS Productivity Handbook: A Statistical Overview and Guide* at www.statistics.gov.uk/about/data/guides/productivity/default.asp

Smith A (1776) 'An Inquiry into the Nature and Causes of the Wealth of Nations', Random House Inc.

APPENDIX

Table A1
Industry descriptions

Description	SIC
Agriculture, hunting, forestry and fishing (AB)	1–5
Mining and quarrying (C)	10–14
Manufacturing (D, 15-37)	
Food, beverages and tobacco	15–16
Textiles, wearing apparel, fur, leather and footwear	17–19
Wood and cork	20
Pulp, paper, printing, publishing and reproduction	21–22
Coke, refined petroleum and nuclear fuel	23
Chemicals and chemical products	24
Rubber and plastics	25
Other non-metallic minerals	26
Basic and fabricated metals	27–28
Machinery	29
Office machinery; electrical machinery; communications equipment; medical instruments	30–33
Motor vehicles and trailers; other transport equipment	34–35
Manufacturing not elsewhere classified; recycling	36–37
Electricity, gas and water (E)	40–41
Construction (F)	45
Services (50+)	
Sale and maintenance of vehicles; retail sale of fuel	50
Wholesale and commission trade, except vehicles	51
Retail trade, except vehicles; repair of household goods	52
Hotels and restaurants (H)	55
Inland, water and air transport; auxiliary transport activities; travel agencies	60–63
Post and telecommunications	64
Financial intermediation; insurance and pensions (J)	65–67
Real estate	70
Renting of machinery and equipment, computer and related; R&D; other business activities	71–74
Public administration and defence (L)	75
Education (M)	80
Health and social work (N)	85
Sewage and refuse; recreational and other service activities (O)	90–93

FEATURE

Rob Luckwell
Office for National Statistics

Producer price index rebasing to 2005=100

SUMMARY

This article describes the effects of rebasing the producer price index onto a 2005=100 base year and briefly summarises the effects that rebasing has on the main headline output and input series of producer prices. The article shows the difference in weighting patterns of both the output and input series of producer prices between the new base year (2005=100) and the previous base year (2000=100). The article also shows a graphical comparison of index values of the main headline series as well as giving a background to producer prices.

The producer price index (PPI) covers four main areas, as indicated in **Table 1**. The new PPI 2005=100 data were published on 13 October 2008. This article is intended to give some background information on the rebasing exercise and was released at the same time, which is consistent with the National Statistics Protocol on Release Practices.

Overview to the changes to the PPI

The PPI has been rebased onto 2005. Rebasing is a five-yearly process for the PPI that updates the weights used to aggregate detailed PPI indices. Further details of the PPI structure and weighting are provided in the Appendix.

With effect from 2005, military products were excluded from the Products of the European Community (PRODCOM) list of questions. As a result, changes have been made to the framework for SIC 2960 (weapons and ammunition), 3511 (ships) and 3530 (aircraft and spacecraft). These changes have no effect on the overall structure of the PPI output series.

Changes to the military series

The decision to exclude military data from PRODCOM caused changes from 2005 to the PRODCOM list. However, PRODCOM decided to continue collecting military sales data but not within the existing question structure. Therefore, to continue collecting military sales, three new PRODCOM headings were created. As the PPI weights are

based on home sales derived from PRODCOM sales, this meant that these changes had to be reflected in the PPI framework for the affected series. As a result, three new military indices have been created in the 2005=100 rebased series to reflect the new PRODCOM questions. In addition, some indices that existed in the 2000=100 series no longer exist in the 2005=100 series or are included in the new military headings. A complete list of indices showing the different structure is available on request.

Rebasing – updating the weights

Updating the base year from the current 2000 to 2005 has led to some changes in weights. The weights at the higher levels have been derived using 2004 Input-Output tables as a proxy for 2005 weights. Current and revised weights for each division within the high net sector output (NSO) level are shown in **Table 2**.

Component weights at this level are based on Input-Output data. The largest differences in weights occur in the alcoholic beverages, clothing, printing and publishing, chemicals and motor vehicles divisions.

Table 1
Main types of PPI series

Description	Index
Gross sector output (GSO)	71xxxxxxxx
Net sector output (NSO)	72xxxxxxxx
Gross sector input (GSI)	61xxxxxxxx
Net sector input (NSI)	62xxxxxxxx

Table 2
Current and revised weights: by division

		Percentages
Component description	2000 weight	2005 weight
Food products excluding beverages	15.0	14.2
Alcoholic beverages	9.3	6.1
Mineral waters and soft drinks	1.3	1.2
Tobacco	3.6	3.1
Textiles	3.1	3.1
Wearing apparel; furs	5.2	6.8
Leather and leather products	0.9	1.7
Wood and products of wood and cork (except furniture), articles of straw and plaiting materials	0.7	1.1
Pulp, paper and paper products	1.9	1.8
Printed matter and recorded media	7.0	5.1
Petroleum	9.1	8.8
Chemicals, chemical products and man-made fibres	5.7	7.7
Rubber and plastic products	2.7	2.8
Other non-metallic mineral products	2.9	2.9
Base metals	0.2	0.2
Fabricated metal products, except machinery and equipment	3.3	2.2
Machinery and equipment n.e.c.	4.5	3.4
Office machinery and computers	1.4	1.5
Electrical machinery and apparatus n.e.c.	1.5	1.3
Radio, television and communication equipment and apparatus	2.9	3.6
Medical precision and optical instruments, watches and clocks	1.8	2.3
Motor vehicles, trailers and semi transport	6.5	8.9
Other transport	1.9	2.5
Other manufactured products including recycling	6.8	6.2
Total	100.0	100.0

Figure 1
Effect of component weight changes to net sector output[1] series

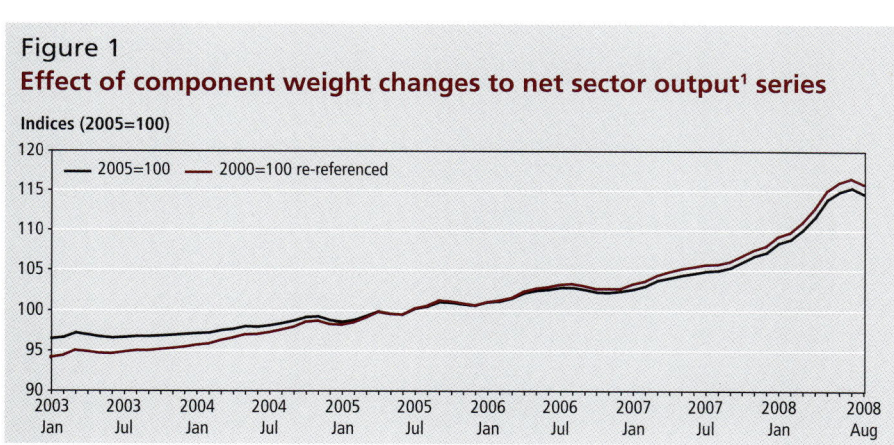

Indices (2005=100)

— 2005=100   — 2000=100 re-referenced

Note:

1   All manufacturing including duty.

Figure 2
Contribution of major components to annual growth in net sector output series

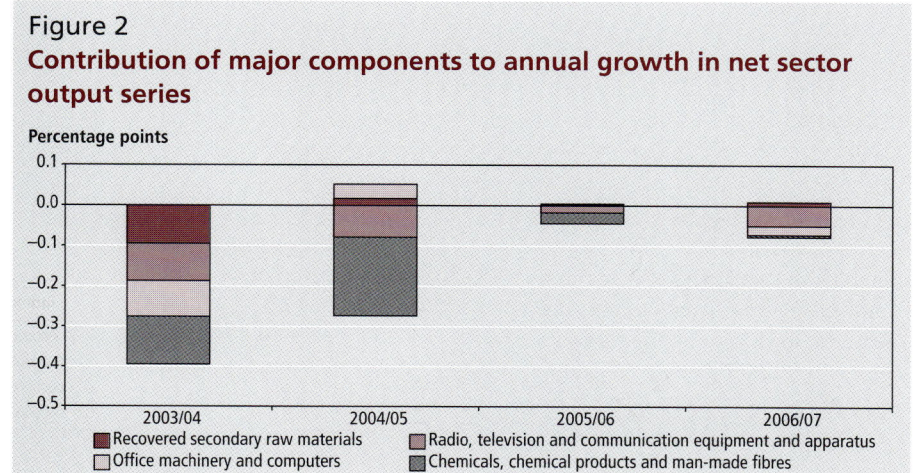

Percentage points

■ Recovered secondary raw materials   ■ Radio, television and communication equipment and apparatus
□ Office machinery and computers   ■ Chemicals, chemical products and man-made fibres

Total effect on net sector output

The effect of the component weight changes to the NSO series is illustrated in **Figure 1**. Here, the 2000-based series (re-referenced to 2005=100 to aid comparison) is compared with the rebased series.

The largest differences are evident in the earlier periods, with differences of around two index points. After 2005, the differences are generally smaller, being around one index point or less. These differences are mainly due to the chemicals; computers; radio, television and communication equipment; and recycling sectors.

Figure 2 shows the contribution these components make to the annual growth in the NSO for the 2005=100 series.

Effect of updating the weights on the input series

Component weights at the high net sector input (NSI) level are based on Input-Output data. **Table 3** shows the commodity groups which make up the high-level NSI series and their respective weights. The largest differences in weight occur in crude oil, food, fuel and other imported parts and equipment divisions.

Total effect on net sector input

The effect of the component weight changes to the NSI series is illustrated in **Figure 3**. Again, the 2000-based series (re-referenced to 2005=100 to aid comparison) is compared with the rebased series.

The largest differences are evident in the earlier periods, with differences of around three index points. In 2004, the differences fall to around one index point, and up to April 2008 they are negligible, falling to less than half an index point. These differences are mainly due to the imported chemicals, home-produced food, imported metals and other home-produced materials sectors.

Conclusion

The overall change to the headline output and input PPIs reflects broadly the same patterns as the 2000=100 series.

Table 3
Current and revised weights: by commodity group

		Percentages
Description	2000 weight	2005 weight
Home-produced and imported crude oil	12.4	19.0
Imported food	4.4	5.5
Other home-produced	1.5	2.9
Imported metals	7.0	6.7
Imported chemicals	13.2	11.4
Fuel including climate change levy	6.9	8.8
Home-produced food	7.8	11.1
Other import commodities	12.8	11.2
Other imports – parts and equipment	34.0	23.4
Total	**100.0**	**100.0**

Figure 3
Effect of component weight changes to net sector input[1] series

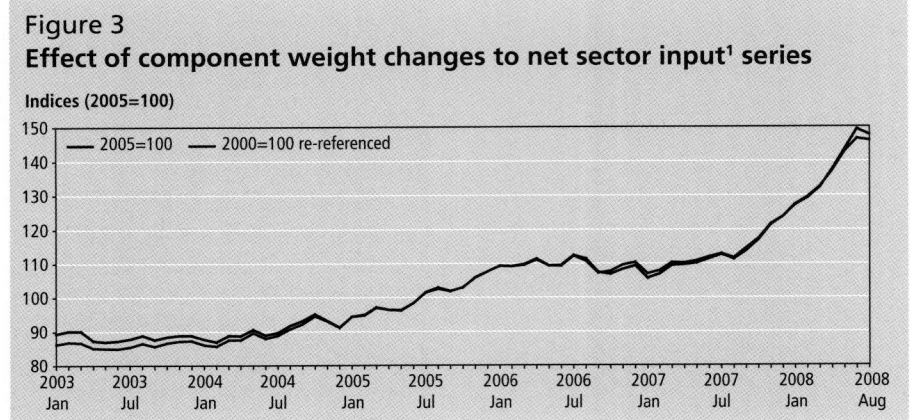

Note:

1   Materials and fuel purchased including climate change levy.

CONTACT

✉ elmr@ons.gsi.gov.uk

Background to producer prices

The PPI measures the change in prices of goods bought and sold by manufacturers. Overall, there are four types of PPI series produced:

- gross sector output (GSO)
- net sector output (NSO)
- gross sector input (GSI), and
- net sector input (NSI)

The differences between output and input prices are:

- output prices – measure the change in price of goods sold by UK manufacturers
- input prices – measure the change in price of goods bought by UK manufacturers for use in the manufacturing process

The differences between net and gross sector are:

- net sector – the weights used to calculate these exclude transactions between companies classified to the same sector, for example, the value of an electronic component manufacturer's sales to a car manufacturer would be excluded from the weights (thereby reflecting the value of sales to purchasers outside the manufacturing sector)
- gross sector – all transactions are included when deriving the weights, including sales within the same sector

The same basic price information is used to feed into each of these four types of PPI series. The difference between the various types lies in the weights that are applied to combine the low-level series to form these higher-level indices and which low-level series are combined to form the high-level indices. The headline series produced in the PPI First Release is the NSO all-manufacturing series including duty.

Price data

Around 6,750 price quotes are collected each month, together with some prices from administrative sources such as trade publications and other government departments. Output PPIs are calculated at a fairly detailed product group (six-digit) level, with the products that fall into each PPI defined by the European Classification of Products by Activity (CPA), which in turn is based on the current 2003 Standard Industrial Classification. Indices produced for 1,270 detailed product groups (six-digit) are then grouped together using the 'family tree' structure of the CPA to produce 237 industry (four-digit) level series. The industry-level series are then grouped to give 24 division-level (two-digit) indices, which in turn are grouped into the all-manufacturing index. An example of this structure is provided in **Figure A1**.

Index weights

The high-level all-manufacturing series are generally structured in the same way. It is easiest to explain the structure for the GSO excluding duty series. Initially, the prices supplied by each contributor are compared with the average price of the same item in the base period, to form a price relative. The price relatives are then weighted together with other products of a similar description to form the six-digit product index. The weights are derived based on the value of the PRODCOM sales (total sales figure obtained from the Products of the European Community survey). The six-digit product groups are then grouped together with the other products of a similar nature to produce the industry indices. In turn, these industries are weighted together to form their retrospective divisional indices. Finally, weighting together all the divisional series then produces the GSO all-manufacturing index.

Indices from product level to divisional level are produced on a gross sector basis. At the all-manufacturing level, output indices are produced on a gross and net sector basis. To calculate the NSO series, the same method is used to produce indices from the product level to generally divisional level as is used for the GSO series. To combine the division-level indices to produce the all-manufacturing NSO series, Input-Output data are used in place of PRODCOM (and export) data to provide index-weighting patterns. Unlike PRODCOM data, which provide only a total product sales value, Input-Output data allow a split in sales to be made within and outside the manufacturing sector, enabling sales to the manufacturing sector to be excluded from the NSO weights.

The NSI series is calculated from import and GSO indices which are calculated up to input/output group level using similar methods to those described above. These series are then weighted together using input/output domestic and import data, removing sales and imports to the manufacturing sector, in the same way as for the NSO series.

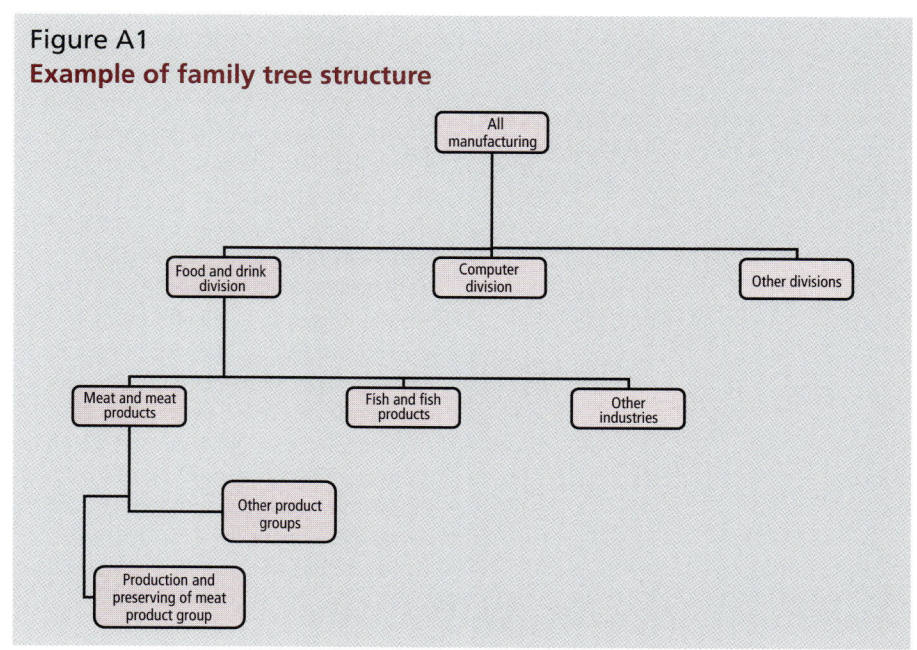

Figure A1
Example of family tree structure

FEATURE

Labour Force Survey: interim reweighting 2008

Nick Palmer and Mark Chandler
Office for National Statistics

SUMMARY

On 15 October 2008, the Office for National Statistics published revised Labour Force Survey (LFS) aggregate estimates in the Labour Market Statistics First Release to take account of the latest available official population estimates. This article describes the new and revised population estimates and the time periods affected. This is supported by tables illustrating the changes at both the total level and by age group. An outline of the reasons for making the revisions and of the basic methodology is then followed by a summary of how the new population figures have impacted on the headline labour market indicators, that is, the measures of UK employment, unemployment and economic activity as derived from the LFS. This includes analysis of revisions arising from the updated seasonal adjustment of the time series. Analysis is also provided of the impact of the revisions to the population estimates by Government Office Region.

On 15 October 2008, revised Labour Force Survey (LFS) estimates, that is, the aggregates in the Labour Market Statistics (LMS) First Release, were published to take into account the latest LFS population data. The LFS data sets used for detailed analysis, known as LFS microdata, are not affected. They continue to be weighted to the population estimates published in the autumn of 2007, as described in Palmer and Hughes (2008). See the following section for the definition of LFS aggregates and microdata.

On 21 August 2008, the Office for National Statistics (ONS) published the 2007 mid-year population estimates for the UK. These were followed by the 2008 Q2 experimental quarterly population estimates (QPEs) for England and Wales on 29 September, which provided new estimates for mid-2008. These new and revised estimates have been incorporated into the calculation of the population figures that have been used to reweight the LFS aggregate estimates.

Defining the LFS aggregate estimates and microdata

The LFS aggregate estimates in the UK and regional Labour Market Statistics First Release are key labour market indicators, for example, the levels and rates of employment, unemployment and economic inactivity. They are derived initially from the LFS microdata and are calculated for any period of three consecutive months. These are referred to as three-month rolling averages, for example, averages for January to March, February to April and so on. The aggregate estimates are seasonally adjusted.

LFS microdata are quarterly data sets containing all survey questions. They are made publicly available as databases to enable external users to access and produce their own analyses. They enable more detailed analysis but are published for calendar quarters only (Q1 refers to January to March, Q2 refers to April to June, and so on), and are not seasonally adjusted.

Background to the LFS

The LFS is a continuous UK household sample survey, which collects information from approximately 53,000 households each quarter (around 110,000 people). Since those responses reflect only a sample (approximately 1 in 500) of the total population, they are weighted on the basis of subnational population totals by age and sex to give estimates for the entire UK household population.

In order to remain consistent with the LFS sample, the population estimates as published are adjusted to exclude those outside the coverage of the LFS. Consequently, people in communal establishments, apart from those living in National Health Service accommodation and students living in halls of residence who have a UK-resident parent, are excluded from the LFS household population estimates. A fuller description of the history of the LFS and its methodology can be found in the Labour Force Survey User Guide Volume 1.

The LFS household population estimates are derived from the annual mid-year population estimates (MYEs) and latest projections based on those MYEs. These are updated annually and thus the LFS aggregate estimates can be revised on a similar basis – see the following section on interim reweighting. Reweighting of the survey microdata to the revised population estimates is a resource-intensive exercise and, historically, has been carried out less frequently than annually. The last full reweighting exercise was carried out in 2007–08 and the results were published on 14 May 2008.

Interim reweighting

Since 2003, the LFS aggregate estimates have been interim reweighted every year. Interim reweighting applies adjustments to the aggregate results to reflect how the latest available LFS household population estimates compare with those used for weighting the microdata. This amounts to an approximation of the effect that a full reweighting of the microdata would have.

The interim reweighting ensures that the time series of the LFS aggregates is kept closely in line with the latest population estimates, thus reflecting a more accurate picture of the UK labour market.

A consequence of this latest interim reweighting of the LFS aggregates in October 2008 is that they are no longer entirely consistent with the quarterly LFS microdata. This applies to all quarterly microdata back to and including July to September 2006. The microdata were last reweighted using the population estimates published in the autumn of 2007 (with results published in May 2008).

Under previous years' interim reweighting, the mid-year population estimate was applied to the June to August three-month period. For the most recent full reweighting of the microdata, the May to July period was used, and this has now been adopted for interim reweighting as well. The main reason for this change was that the May to July period appeared to be the more intuitive of the two possibilities, although both are equally valid statistically.

LFS household population estimates

The official population estimates published in August and September 2008 indicate that the previously published population projection for mid-2007 was very accurate as a predictor of the MYE. The estimate of LFS household population for people aged 16 and over for mid-2007, derived from the

2007 MYE, was just 4,000 lower than that derived from the previous year's projection. The difference between the latest and previous estimate for mid-2008 is slightly larger at –53,000, or –0.1 per cent, but this is still relatively small when compared with previous years' revisions.

Table 1 compares the new LFS household population estimates by age group with those previously used.

There were no revisions to the MYEs prior to 2007; therefore, the LFS aggregates are open to revision for the period June to August 2006 onwards.

The main driver of the revision to mid-2008 estimates is a downward revision of 47,000 to the estimate of the number of females aged 25 to 34. This is mainly due to revised projections for the migration component for females, as reflected in the QPEs for 2008.[1]

Revisions to LFS aggregates

The remainder of this article will examine the impact of the interim reweighting on the headline aggregates by labour market status.

The interim reweighting of the seasonally adjusted aggregates includes revisions arising purely from the seasonal adjustment. This is partly because previously published LFS aggregate estimates are not routinely revised, in accordance with the published revisions policy for Labour Market Statistics.[2] This means that they each reflect the seasonal adjustment of the time series that existed at the time they were first published. The LFS aggregates are interim reweighted prior to being seasonally adjusted and then a fully revised time series is fed into the seasonal adjustment process. Consequently, the seasonally adjusted estimates for all periods open to revision reflect the most up-to-date estimation of the seasonal factors, trends and irregular components as required.

In previous years, the interim reweighting of the LFS aggregates has coincided with the implementation of the annual review of the seasonal adjustment of the LFS. The most recent detailed review was carried out in spring 2008 and the outcome was summarised in the reweighting article published in June 2008. This review is sufficiently up to date and consequently there have been no further changes to the way the LFS aggregate estimates are seasonally adjusted.

The largest revisions caused by the interim reweighting of the LFS aggregate estimates were mainly to the most recently published period, May to July 2008. This is primarily because the revisions to the LFS household population estimates get progressively larger from mid-2006 onwards. The revisions to the headline figures for this period are summarised in **Table 2**.

Generally, since the population revisions are included in both the numerator and denominator for the rate calculations, the revisions to the rates are very small, that is, less than 0.1 percentage points and, in many cases, zero. Consequently, the comparisons in this article focus on the levels rather than rates.

Table 3 shows the revisions resulting from interim reweighting for the main LFS aggregates, by age group. The relative sizes of the revisions tend to reflect the population revisions by age group, as shown in Table 1.

For the economically active, in employment and economically inactive series, the revisions result almost entirely from the latest LFS household population estimates only. In other words, the effects from the updated seasonal adjustment are minimal for those series. For the unemployment series, however, the opposite is true, and more detail is given in the section on unemployment estimates.

Table 1
New and previous LFS household population estimates: by age band

United Kingdom								Thousands, except where indicated
	May to July 2007				May to July 2008			
Age band	New	Previous	Revision	Percentage revision	New	Previous	Revision	Percentage revision
16+	48,654	48,659	−4	–	49,039	49,092	−53	−0.1
16–59/64	37,560	37,574	−15	–	37,731	37,774	−44	−0.1
16–17	1,588	1,589	−1	−0.1	1,591	1,583	7	0.5
18–24	5,640	5,640	–	–	5,744	5,732	13	0.2
25–34	7,780	7,792	−11	−0.1	7,805	7,854	−48	−0.6
35–49	13,424	13,417	7	0.1	13,438	13,435	3	–
50–59/64	9,128	9,137	−9	−0.1	9,152	9,171	−19	−0.2
60/65+	11,094	11,084	10	0.1	11,308	11,317	−9	−0.1

Source: Office for National Statistics

Table 2
Revisions to headline LFS aggregates, May to July 2008

United Kingdom   Thousands, except where indicated

	New	Previous	Revision	Percentage revision
People aged 16+				
Economically active	31,219	31,262	−44	−0.1
In employment	29,491	29,538	−47	−0.2
Unemployed	1,727	1,724	3	0.2
Economically inactive	17,820	17,829	−9	−0.1
Working-age people[1]				
Economically active	29,870	29,911	−41	−0.1
In employment	28,165	28,209	−44	−0.2
Unemployed	1,705	1,702	3	0.2
Economically inactive	7,860	7,863	−3	–

Note: *Source: Office for National Statistics*

1   Men aged 16 to 64 and women aged 16 to 59.

Table 3
Revisions: by economic activity status and age group, May to July 2008

United Kingdom   Thousands

Age group	Economically active	In employment	Unemployed	Economically inactive
16–17	2	2	–	6
18–24	10	7	4	3
25–34	−39	−41	1	−9
35–49	1	–	–	3
50–59/64	−14	−12	−2	−5
60/65+	−3	−3	–	−6

Source: Office for National Statistics

Unemployment estimates

The interim-reweighted aggregate estimates of the level of unemployment for people aged 16 and over mainly reflect the updated seasonal adjustment. The revisions resulting purely from the revised LFS household population estimates, that is, before seasonal adjustment, were negligible. The revisions relate primarily to updated seasonal factors over the last two years, which are estimated as part of the normal seasonal adjustment process. The revisions to the seasonally adjusted figures are upwards from October to December 2007 to April to June 2008 and downwards from May to July 2007 to September to November 2007, as illustrated in **Figure 1**. The revisions range from +13,000 (+0.8 per cent) in February to April 2008 to −14,000 (−0.8 per cent) in July to September 2007.

Revisions by Government Office Region

Figure 2 shows the revisions to the May to July 2008 LFS household population estimates for people aged 16 and over, broken down by Government Office Region.

The largest revisions were downward ones of 17,000 for the North West and for London. The largest upward revision was for the South West, at 11,000. In percentage

terms, the revisions to the LFS household population for people aged 16 and over for all regions were between −0.3 and +0.3 per cent.

Table 4 shows the revisions arising from interim reweighting for the main LFS aggregates, by region. As for the age group breakdown, the revisions to the results generally reflect quite closely the revisions to the estimates of the LFS household population.

Conclusion

The LFS aggregate estimates for key labour market indicators have been interim reweighted to bring them into line with the latest official population estimates. There are no significant revisions to the headline figures and no changes to the statistical story presented by those figures.

The full set of interim-reweighted aggregates is included in the Labour Market Statistics First Release and supplementary tables, as published on 15 October 2008.

ONS aims to ensure that its published LFS estimates continue to be kept closely in line with the latest population estimates. Future revised population estimates will be incorporated into the revised LFS series using the interim LFS adjustment

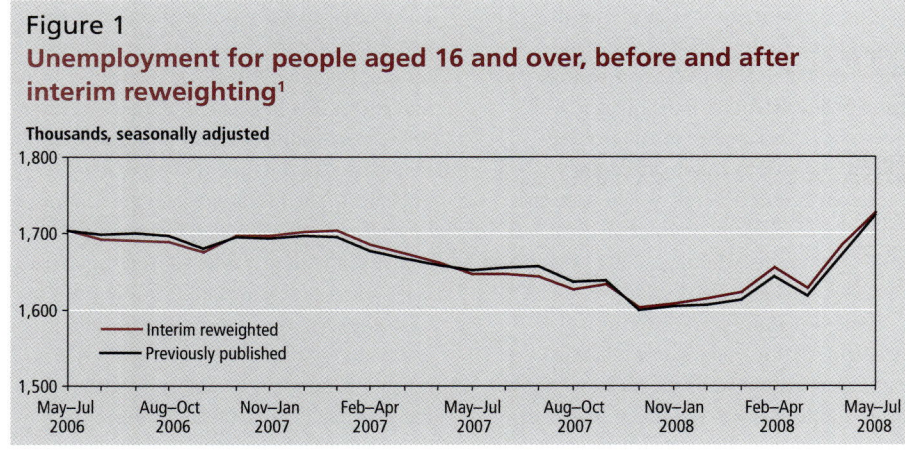

Figure 1
Unemployment for people aged 16 and over, before and after interim reweighting[1]

Note:

1   Rolling three-month periods, May to July 2006 to May to July 2008.

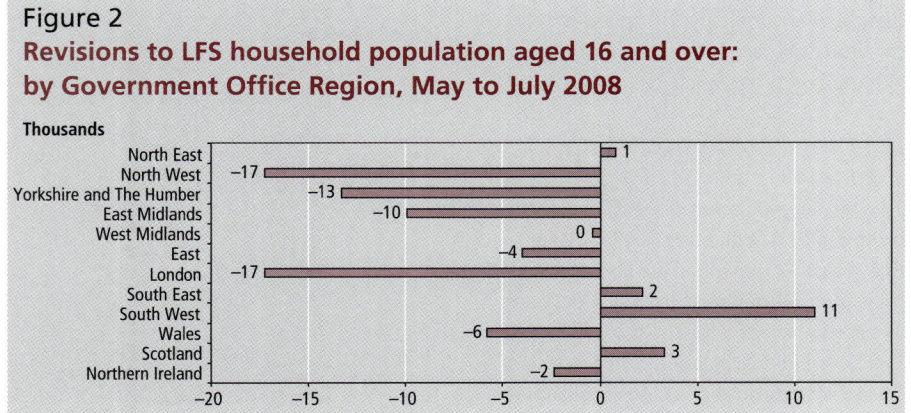

Figure 2
Revisions to LFS household population aged 16 and over: by Government Office Region, May to July 2008

Table 4

Changes as a result of latest revisions: by economic activity status and Government Office Region, May to July 2008

| | | | | Thousands |
Government Office Region	Economically active	In employment	Unemployed	Economically inactive
North East	1	−1	2	−
North West	−15	−14	−1	−2
Yorkshire and The Humber	−8	−7	−1	−5
East Midlands	−8	−7	−1	−2
West Midlands	1	1	−	−1
East	−5	−6	2	1
London	−19	−19	1	1
South East	1	2	−2	1
South West	6	6	1	5
Wales	−	−2	2	−6
Scotland	5	5	1	−2
Northern Ireland	−1	−1	−	−1

Source: Office for National Statistics

procedure, as appropriate. Full reweighting of the LFS microdata in future years will depend on the extent of revisions to official population estimates and the availability of resources.

Notes

1   See www.statistics.gov.uk/statbase/ product.asp?vlnk=13523
2   See www.statistics.gov.uk/about/ methodology_by_theme/downloads/ lm_revisionspolicy.pdf

CONTACT

 elmr@ons.gsi.gov.uk

REFERENCES

Palmer N and Hughes M (2008) 'Labour Force Survey: reweighting and seasonal adjustment review 2008', *Economic & Labour Market Review* 2(6), pp 33–42 and at www.statistics.gov.uk/cci/article.asp?id=2011

FEATURE

Sumit Dey-Chowdhury
Department for Business, Enterprise & Regulatory Reform (formerly Office for National Statistics)

Pippa Gibson
Department for Environment, Food and Rural Affairs

Experimental estimates of rural-urban productivity

SUMMARY

Understanding the economic performance of rural areas is an important part of government policy. This article presents experimental estimates of productivity at the rural and urban level for England as a result of collaboration between the Office for National Statistics and the Department for Environment, Food and Rural Affairs. These estimates, which are available from 2002 to 2005 and which will be produced in spring each year, have been developed to allow policy analysts and others to better measure the economic performance of rural and urban areas in England than is possible with existing regional productivity figures, which do not provide the necessary level of detail. The article outlines the underlying methodology and presents some of the key results.

The Government's central economic objective is to achieve high and stable rates of economic growth and employment. Productivity growth, alongside high and stable levels of employment, is central to long-term economic performance and rising living standards. The economic performance of rural areas is an important aspect of the commitment by the Department for Environment, Food and Rural Affairs (Defra) to sustain strong rural communities, as outlined in its Rural Strategy in 2004.[1] One of the priorities set out in the Rural Strategy concerns economic and social regeneration – supporting enterprise across rural England, but targeting greater resources at areas of greatest need. Rural economic performance has been integral to Defra's rural indicators ever since. To identify variance in performance between different types of areas, it is important to use a robust and recognised measure of productivity. Furthermore, when examining productivity in rural areas, it is essential that estimates are available at least at local authority district (LAD) level, as these are the largest geographical areas to which a rural classification can be applied (see **Box 1**). This gives a picture of rural and urban performance compared with the national average, which can help facilitate greater understanding of economic performance in terms of productivity in areas with different levels of rurality.

During the Spending Review period 2004 to 2008, one of Defra's Public Service Agreements (PSAs) aimed to 'enhance opportunity and tackle social exclusion in rural areas'. The relevant PSA target was to:

reduce the gap in productivity between the least well performing quartile of rural areas and the English median by 2008, demonstrating progress by 2006, and improve the accessibility of services for people in rural areas.

The indicator developed to measure productivity for this PSA was based on average employment income weighted by employment rate. While this gave an indication of economic performance, it was not a direct measure of productivity that was consistent with official methods of estimating productivity.

For the current Comprehensive Spending Review period (2008–11), Defra's new Departmental Strategic Objective (DSO) for 'Strong Rural Communities' aims, in part, at economic growth being supported in rural areas with the lowest levels of performance.[2] An essential foundation of this indicator is a robust measure of labour productivity, with a methodology consistent with official measures of regional productivity published by the Office for National Statistics (ONS). Following collaboration between Defra's Rural Statistics Unit and ONS, a new methodology has been developed to produce experimental estimates of productivity at the rural-urban level that will be used to assess performance against this objective.

The rest of this article outlines this new

Box 1

Defining 'rural' at district level

The Rural/Urban Definition, an official National Statistic introduced in 2004, defines the rurality of small census geographies such as census output areas and wards. Areas forming settlements with populations of over 10,000 are urban, while the remainder are defined as rural town and fringe, village or hamlet and dispersed.

This definition forms the basis of the LAD Rural Urban classification system, constructed by the Rural Evidence Research Centre at Birkbeck College. The categories of the classification and criteria for identifying them are as follows:

- major urban (MU) – districts with either 100,000 people or 50 per cent of their population living in urban areas with a population of more than 750,000. There are 76 districts in this group, with an aggregate population at the 2001 Census of 17.2 million

- large urban (LU) – districts with either 50,000 people or 50 per cent of their population living in one of 17 urban areas with a population between 250,000 and 750,000. There are 45 districts in this group, with an aggregate population of 7.3 million

- other urban (OU) – districts with fewer than 37,000 people and less than 26 per cent of their population living in rural settlements and larger market towns.[3] There are 55 districts in this group, with an aggregate population of 6.7 million

- significant rural (SR) – districts with more than 37,000 people or more than 26 per cent of their population living in rural settlements and larger market towns. There are 53 districts in this group, with an aggregate population of 6.4 million

- rural-50 (R50) – districts with at least 50 per cent but less than 80 per cent of their population living in rural settlements and larger market towns. There are 52 districts in this group, with an aggregate population of 5.8 million, and

- rural-80 (R80) – districts with at least 80 per cent of their population living in rural settlements and larger market towns. There are 73 districts in this group, with an aggregate population of 5.7 million

These classifications form the basis of the experimental estimates of rural-urban productivity that are presented here.[4]

methodology in more detail, and presents some of the key results. The article then concludes with how these results can be used in a policy context and proposes future developments.

Methodology

Estimates of regional productivity at the NUTS 1 level are published annually by ONS. The NUTS 1 regions for the UK are the nine English Government Office Regions (North East, North West, Yorkshire and The Humber, East Midlands, West Midlands, East of England, London, South East and South West) plus Scotland, Wales and Northern Ireland. The regional productivity estimates are available on an output per filled job basis. These are published as indices relative to the UK average, where the UK is equal to 100, with the difference between the region and the UK a measure of the regional productivity gap. Following the methodology changes that came into effect from February 2008 (see Dey-Chowdhury et al 2008), unsmoothed estimates of gross value added (GVA) are used as the output measure. The input of labour is measured by the workforce jobs (WFJ) series, which estimates the number of jobs by region. In deriving these experimental estimates of productivity at the rural-urban level, these data sources and the methodology were followed as closely as possible.

The estimates presented in this article are for England only. In order to produce these experimental estimates at the rural-urban level, it is necessary to first derive estimates

of both GVA and WFJ at the LAD level, using a top-down approach from the nine English Government Office Regions, and then aggregate up from these 354 English LADs to the six categories of the LAD classification (a bottom-up approach). As outlined in Box 1, each English LAD has its own classification, which means that it is possible to map directly from the LAD level to the rural-urban classification that is presented here.

Estimates of regional GVA are published for each of the NUTS 1, 2 and 3 regions. In order to derive estimates at the LAD level, published unsmoothed GVA estimates at the NUTS 3 level were allocated down to the LADs that comprise a particular NUTS 3 region. For example, the published GVA estimate for the NUTS 3 region West Cumbria was split and allocated to the corresponding LADs of Allerdale, Barrow-in-Furness and Copeland. The basis of this allocation was GVA data obtained from the Annual Business Inquiry (ABI). The ABI is just one source that is used to compile the published estimates of regional GVA, and has the advantage of being available at the LAD level. Although the totals differ (see **Box 2** for details), these data can still be used to construct GVA-based weights to split the published NUTS 3 estimates. One advantage of this approach is that these weights are being applied to the published totals, ensuring complete consistency with the headline estimates of regional GVA.

Since WFJ data are publicly available at the LAD level, this means that the input

data at this level are constrained with published data at the NUTS 1 level. (Note that the published estimates are rounded to the nearest thousand, so the LAD estimates are constrained to the more detailed NUTS 1 estimates to ensure complete consistency.) Although the underlying input data are consistent with those used to construct headline estimates of regional productivity, the productivity estimates in this article are indexed relative to the England average (so that England is equal to 100) rather than the UK average, as is done in official publications.

Results

This section of the article presents the main findings, and thereby seeks to determine whether the economic performance of rural areas is relatively worse than that of urban areas and the national average, and whether this has changed over the last few years.[5]

Figure 1 shows estimates of output per job for 2005 for the six categories of the LAD classification. Due to the experimental nature of these estimates (and specifically the use of ABI data at such a low regional level), it is advised that differences of a few percentage points are not seen as significant as they could be due to measurement issues. This follows a similar recommendation that ONS uses when making international comparisons of productivity (see ONS 2007a). Figure 1 shows that, whereas there is a significant productivity gap between major urban areas and England as a whole (and likewise between rural-80

Box 2

Estimates of regional GVA

ONS currently only uses the income approach to produce its headline estimates of regional GVA. This involves adding up all the forms of income earned in the region in the production of goods and services. Several data sources (including the ABI) are used to produce the components of the income measure of regional GVA. These are available for all NUTS 1, 2 and 3 regions and are allocated to each region using the most appropriate set of available indicators, which are based on a combination of survey and administrative sources (Holmes 2008). These estimates are based on a top-down approach, as national

aggregates are allocated down to the regional level using the relevant indicator of regional activity.

The ABI estimates of regional GVA, which were used to construct weights to apportion the NUTS 3 estimates of GVA to the LAD level, differ from the headline estimates that are published. These are based on only this one data source, and are derived using the production approach. This approach measures the value of output of goods and services produced, removing the value of intermediate consumption. In addition, the ABI data are not subject to adjustments required to make them consistent with the European System of Accounts 95.

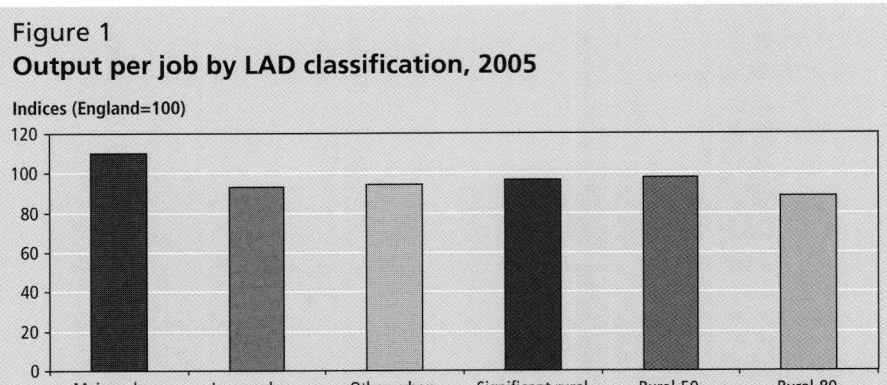

Figure 1
Output per job by LAD classification, 2005

Indices (England=100)

LADs and England), it is not possible to distinguish productivity levels for the other four categories of the LAD classification. This shows that there is no discernable rural-urban productivity gap, except at the extreme end of the LAD classification – major urban and rural-80 LADs.

While the analysis above assesses whether productivity gaps (in terms of levels) exist between rural and urban areas, it is also important to consider whether such gaps have changed over time. Policies are often focused over the long- to medium-term, as is the case in the Defra DSO. **Figure 2** shows rural-urban productivity estimates over the period 2002 to 2005. It should be noted, however, that comparisons of growth between rural-urban categories should not be made because the estimates of GVA used in calculating these productivity estimates are in nominal, not real, terms. Currently, regional price deflators do not exist, so it is not possible to isolate volume changes from price changes. In terms of output growth, it is only the former that are of interest.

Figure 2 shows that there have not been any discernable changes in the productivity gaps observed in 2005 from earlier years. Although the productivity performance of rural-80 LADs seems to have improved between 2002 and 2005, it is not possible

to say whether this improvement is an actual productivity improvement or whether it is an apparent change caused by measurement-related issues. To carry out more meaningful time series analysis, a longer time series should be assessed. This is currently being developed.

Looking at the productivity estimates at the LAD level, there seems to be a 'London' effect in that a significant proportion of the major urban areas, which have been shown to perform well on this indicator, are London-based. This can be seen by the concentrated area of LADs around London, whose productivity is significantly greater than that for England as a whole. This raises the question of what is driving the productivity gap that is observed between

major urban LADs and England: is it due to these areas being urban or mainly due to the performance of London?

Since the LADs that comprise London are all defined as major urban, it is possible to separate out the London-based major urban LADs. The results are summarised in **Figure 3**.

Figure 3 shows that an important factor behind the productivity gap seen earlier for major urban local authorities is that many of the major urban LADs are London-based – 33 of the 76 English major urban LADs. When London is separated from the other major urban areas, it is not possible to distinguish the economic performance of these areas from the other categories of the LAD classification; there is no rural-urban productivity gap if London is excluded. This analysis shows that major urban LADs are not necessarily more productive, rather that there is a specific 'London' effect.

Economic theory suggests that there may be reasons why cities tend to perform better economically than rural areas. Agglomeration effects or 'clustering' describe the forces that make firms in places of dense economic activities, such as cities, especially productive. Ciccone (2001) analyses the role of agglomeration effects in explaining differences in regional productivity across Europe and the United

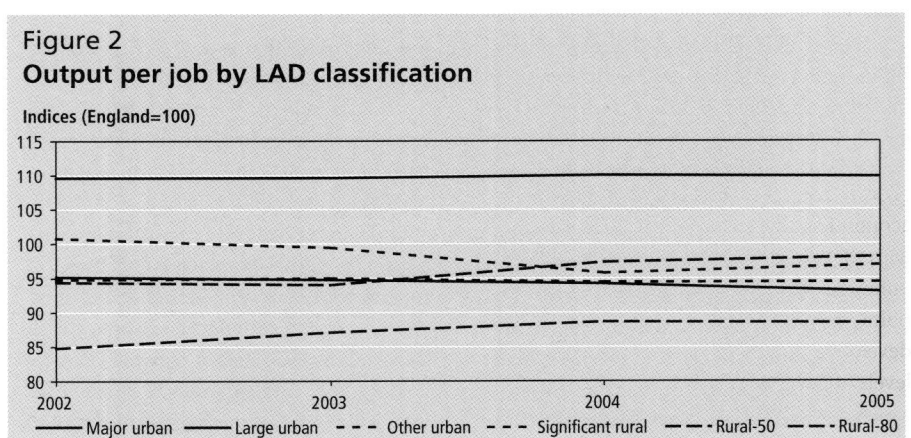

Figure 2
Output per job by LAD classification

Indices (England=100)

Major urban —— Large urban —— Other urban – – – Significant rural – – – Rural-50 — — — Rural-80 — — —

Figure 3
Output per job, treating London-based major urban LADs separately, 2005

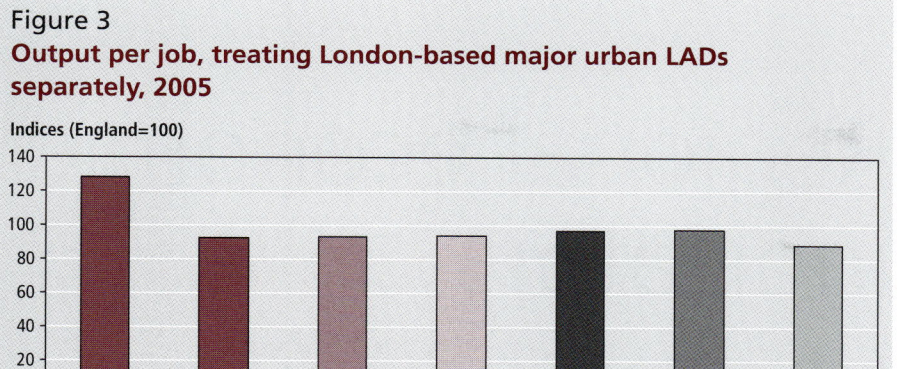

Indices (England=100)

Office for National Statistics (2007a) *The ONS Productivity Handbook: A Statistical Overview and Guide* at www.statistics.gov.uk/about/data/guides/productivity/default.asp

Office for National Statistics (2007b) *Regional Accounts Methodology Guide* at www.statistics.gov.uk/downloads/theme_economy/regionalaccountsmethodologyguide.pdf

States. Ciccone concludes that a large part of regional productivity differences can be explained by agglomeration effects. The analysis of the experimental estimates presented here shows that there is a London capital city effect, which may be being driven by agglomeration effects.

Conclusion

This article outlines developmental work carried out by ONS and Defra to improve the measurement of labour productivity at the rural-urban level, which has helped better assess any productivity differential between rural and urban areas. This is in line with the DSO for which Defra is responsible. The main findings of this work are that a productivity gap does exist between major urban LADs and England as a whole, which has not changed considerably between 2002 and 2005. However, much of this gap is driven by the performance of London. If London is excluded from the analysis, there is little, if any, productivity gap between urban and rural areas.

Going forward, these experimental statistics can be useful in dialogue with regional partners, where the figures can be used to identify relatively strong and weak economic areas and as the basis for exploring the underlying factors behind such differences. By updating the figures each spring, a longer time series will be established and genuine decreases and increases in the productivity gap between rural or urban LADs and the national average will be identified. Further analysis might also compare the economic performance of city regions with that of London. In terms of rural policy, using these estimates as a starting point, approaches to supporting economic development in rural areas with the lowest levels of performance will be able to be assessed more thoroughly.

Notes

1   See www.defra.gov.uk/rural/strategy/default.htm

2   See www.defra.gov.uk/rural/dso/index.htm

3   Certain urban areas with between 10,000 and 30,000 population are identified as 'larger market towns' and are taken into account in assessing the rurality of a district. Such towns are identified by the presence of a prescribed set of services and commercial attributes. Here, the populations of 207 'larger market towns' contribute to the rural population of the districts in which they are located, although within the Rural/Urban Definition they are defined as urban and their populations are not included in the rural domain.

4   For more detailed methodological information, see www.defra.gov.uk/rural/ruralstats/rural-definition.htm

5   Detailed estimates can be obtained at www.defra.gov.uk/rural/dso/productivity/index.htm

CONTACT

 elmr@ons.gsi.gov.uk

REFERENCES

Ciccone A (2001) 'Agglomeration Effects in Europe and the USA' available at www.crei.cat/research/opuscles/op9ang.pdf

Dey-Chowdhury S, Penny D, Walker M and Wosnitza B (2008) 'Regional economic indicators, February 2008, with a focus on regional productivity', *Economic & Labour Market Review* 2(2), pp 48–61 and at www.statistics.gov.uk/cci/article.asp?id=1945

Holmes E (2008) 'Regional gross value added', *Economic & Labour Market Review* 2(3), pp 44–54 and at www.statistics.gov.uk/cci/article.asp?id=1954

FEATURE

Birgit Wosnitza, Peggy Causer and Jonathan Knight
Office for National Statistics

Regional economic indicators November 2008
with a focus on skills

SUMMARY

This quarter, the Regional economic indicators (REI) article focuses on skills – one of the drivers of regional productivity. The regular part of the article then gives an overview of the economic activity of UK regions in terms of their GVA, their GVA per head and their labour productivity. This is followed by a presentation of headline indicators of regional welfare, other drivers of regional productivity and regional labour market statistics. The indicators cover the nine Government Office Regions of England and the devolved administrations of Northern Ireland, Scotland and Wales. These 12 areas comprise level 1 of the European Nomenclature of Units for Territorial Statistics (NUTS level 1) for the UK. The term 'region' is used to describe this level of geography for convenience in the rest of this article.

Focus on skills

This article focuses on skills, one of the key drivers of productivity as defined by HM Treasury and the Department for Business, Enterprise & Regulatory Reform (BERR). The skills of workers influence productivity as they define the capabilities that the labour force can contribute to the production process. The concept of skills includes attributes of the workforce, such as 'softer' or interpersonal skills, which are difficult to measure or to compare in different situations or over time. Therefore, qualifications are often used as proxy indicators. By examining the qualifications of the current workforce as well as those of young people, who represent the future capabilities of the labour market, a view of how skills are changing over time and the potential impact on productivity can be obtained.

The latest estimate of the highest qualifications of the working-age population (currently defined as males aged 16 to 64 and females aged 16 to 59) are based on the second quarter 2008 Labour Force Survey (LFS) estimates. **Table 1** shows that overall around one-fifth of the working-age population had a degree or equivalent qualification in the second quarter of 2008. A summary of equivalent levels of qualifications can be found in the 'Notes and definitions: Education & Training' webpages on the ONS Regional Snapshot (www.statistics. gov.uk/statbase/Product.asp?vlnk=14712). London had the highest proportion (about 32 per cent) of people between 16 and state pension age with a degree or equivalent, although the region had well below average proportions with GCSEs or A levels. As characteristics of local economies dictate which labour skills are required, comparability between regions might be difficult. An alternative approach is to compare the percentage of the working-age population that has no recognised qualifications.

Figure 1 compares the proportions of the working-age population that have no qualifications in each region against the UK average for the second quarter of 2008. Northern Ireland had the highest proportion of population with no qualifications (9.5 percentage points above the UK average), whereas the South West and the South East had the lowest proportions, 3.8 and 3.4 percentage points respectively below the UK average.

Above average proportions of working-age people without a qualification do not necessarily mean that regions have the most unqualified workforce. A reason for this might be the differing regional skill requirements, which might induce a significant number of those with qualifications to migrate into other regions. At the same time those without qualifications might have migrated out of these other regions. Employer demand can also influence the regional pattern, that is, there may be strong demand for lower skills from employers and a good supply of appropriate workers in the region, creating a low skill equilibrium.

Table 1
Working-age population[1] by highest qualification:[2,3] by NUTS1 region, second quarter 2008

Percentages

	Degree or equivalent	Higher education qualifications below degree	GCE A level or equivalent & apprenticeships	GCSE grades A* to C or equivalent	Other qualifications	No qualifications
United Kingdom	20.3	8.4	23.2	22.7	12.8	12.6
North East	14.5	7.3	26.4	25.4	11.8	14.6
North West	17.4	9.1	23.3	25.4	10.8	14.0
Yorkshire and The Humber	17.2	7.4	23.7	23.3	14.5	13.8
East Midlands	16.2	8.0	23.7	24.1	15.5	12.5
West Midlands	16.8	7.8	22.2	24.8	12.3	16.2
East of England	18.7	7.6	23.6	24.7	13.7	11.7
London	31.9	5.8	16.3	15.8	18.2	11.9
South East	22.0	8.7	24.1	23.7	12.3	9.2
South West	19.4	9.4	26.5	24.5	11.5	8.8
England	20.5	7.9	22.7	23.0	13.6	12.3
Wales	18.1	8.8	22.1	25.8	10.4	14.8
Scotland	20.2	13.3	27.8	18.4	8.5	11.8
Northern Ireland	19.2	7.5	24.4	21.0	5.8	22.1

Notes:

Source: Labour Force Survey, Office for National Statistics

1 Males aged 16 to 64 and females aged 16 to 59.
2 For summary of qualifications and equivalents, see www.statistics.gov.uk/statbase/Product.asp?vlnk=14712
3 See Technical Note for information on the confidence intervals around the estimates.

Table 2
Regional Skills Partnerships core indicators: by NUTS1 region

	Time period	Units	North East	North West	Yorkshire and The Humber	East Midlands	West Midlands	East of England	London	South East	South West	England
Contextual indicators												
GVA per hour worked	2006	UK=100	93.4	90.8	90.6	96.7	91.0	98.5	123.1	108.3	96.7	101.6
Unemployment rate (ILO definition)	Jan-Dec 2007	%	6.3	5.8	5.6	5.1	6.1	4.5	6.9	4.3	4.1	5.4
Employment rate (working age)	Jan-Dec 2007	%	71.6	72.3	73.2	75.9	72.4	77.4	69.8	78.4	78.2	74.4
Median gross weekly earnings (full-time)	Apr-07	£	402.90	434.20	422.30	420.20	430.00	450.00	580.90	480.70	427.80	462.00
New VAT-registered businesses per 10,000 adult population	2006	Rate	22	32	31	35	34	39	57	43	37	39
Skills outcome indicators												
Percentage of employers with business or training plan, or budget for training	2007	%	70.6	69.2	69.6	67.9	67.5	67.3	70.0	70.6	68.4	69.1
Percentage of staff with skill gaps	2007	%	6.3	5.3	4.8	6.8	5.4	7.8	6.7	5.8	6.2	6.1
Skill shortage vacancies as percentage of all vacancies	2007	%	18.8	17.6	20.1	20.2	15.5	19.6	26.1	22.5	20.9	20.9
Percentage of pupils achieving 5+ A* to C GCSE (inc Maths and English)	2007/08[1]	%	44.6	46.9	43.9	46.5	45.7	50.0	49.8	51.4	49.0	47.9
Percentage of 19 year olds qualified to Level 2 or above	2007	%	73.2	72.4	69.9	71.2	72.1	74.7	74.1	77.6	76.1	73.9
Percentage of 19 year olds qualified to Level 3 or above	2007	%	41.6	44.6	42.8	44.5	45.8	49.6	50.5	55.3	50.2	48.0
Percentage of 19 to state pension age with Level 2+	2007	%	69.3	67.7	65.8	67.2	65.4	67.0	70.3	72.6	72.5	68.9
Percentage of 19 to state pension age with Level 3+	2007	%	47.1	46.8	45.0	47.0	44.8	46.2	54.1	52.7	52.2	49.0
Percentage of 19 to state pension age with Level 4+	2007	%	25.9	27.1	25.4	27.3	26.3	27.7	39.4	32.9	31.0	30.2
Percentage of 19 to state pension age with no qualifications	2007	%	13.4	14.5	14.0	13.1	16.5	11.9	12.4	9.2	8.9	12.5
Percentage of working-age population who undertook job-related training in last 13 weeks	2007	%	23.1	19.5	19.6	20.7	20.1	19.4	18.8	21.5	22.0	20.3
Percentage of 17 year olds in education or work-based learning	End-2006	%	76.0	77.0	73.0	74.0	77.0	76.0	85.0	78.0	76.0	77.0

Note:

Source: Labour Force Survey, Office for National Statistics; Department for Business, Enterprise & Regulatory Reform; Department for Children, Schools and Families; Department for Innovation, Universities and Skills; National Employers Skills Survey 2007

1 Provisional data.

Figure 1
Working-age population with no qualifications: by NUTS1 region, second quarter 2008

Source: Labour Force Survey, Office for National Statistics

Figure 2
Percentage of people aged 19 to state pension age, qualified to at least level 4: by NUTS1 region

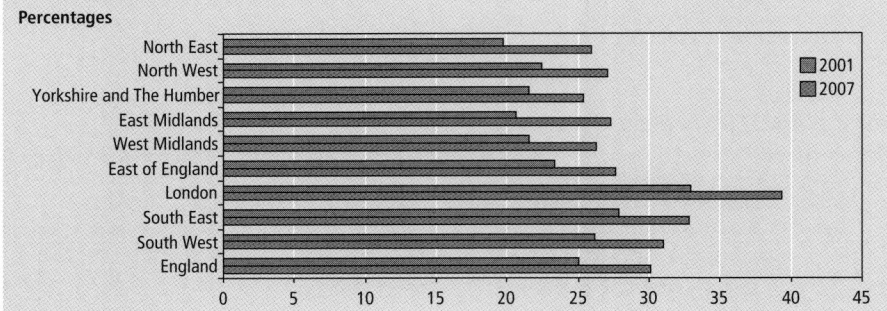

Source: Labour Force Survey, Office for National Statistics

Table 2 shows a selection of indicators, which have been agreed by a cross-regional group representing the Regional Skills Partnerships (RSPs). These partnerships are groups brought together by Regional Development Agencies in each region of England in response to the National Skills Strategy and comprise organisations such as the Skills for Business Network, Learning and Skills Council (LSC), Small Business Service and Jobcentre Plus among others. RSPs aim to strengthen regional structures to make skills provision more relevant to the needs of employers and individuals, covering private, public and voluntary sectors of the economy. They also aim to give regions the flexibility to tackle their own individual challenges and priorities.

The indicators in Table 2 will assist the RSPs to monitor the health of regional and local labour markets in their areas and progress towards national skills targets such as documented in the Leitch Report. These core indicators, which include some of the contextual information already contained in the regular part of this article, will be supported by local, more specific, indicators identified by individual RSPs. The choice

of '19 to state pension age' for some of the indicators in Table 2 has been influenced by these factors: the increased emphasis on education and training after the age of 16; the plan to raise the standard school leaving age to 18; and alignment with indicators specified in the local area agreements (LAAs).

Figure 2 shows the changes in proportion of the population between 19 and state pension age qualified to NVQ level 4 or higher. In London nearly 40 per cent of people aged 19 to pension age had achieved

equivalent to at least NVQ level 4 by 2007, which marks an increase of 6.5 percentage points since 2001. Yorkshire and The Humber had the lowest proportion in 2007, at roughly 25 per cent, with an increase of 3.8 percentage points over the same period. The greatest improvement in the proportion of people aged 19 to pension age attaining NVQ level 4 or above was in the East Midlands, with an increase of 6.6 percentage points; the North East also showed above average improvement of more than 6 percentage points.

The North East also had the largest reduction in people aged 19 to pension age with no qualification, at over 6 percentage points, as can be seen in **Figure 3**. In 2001, almost one-fifth of people between 19 and pension age in the North East had no qualifications, the joint highest with the West Midlands. London showed the least reduction, 1.7 percentage points, in the proportion of adults with no formal qualifications between 2001 and 2007.

Since 2003, the LSC alongside its partners, the Department for Innovation, Universities and Skills (DIUS) (previously part of the Department for Education and Skills DfES) and the former Sector Skills Development Agency (now UKCES) have commissioned the National Employers Skills Surveys (NESS). The survey covers over 79,000 employers in England and thus represents a comprehensive source of reliable information on current skills issues affecting employers. It is a key source of labour market information on skill-shortage vacancies, skills gaps and workforce development activity, and is a crucial part of the evidence to inform skills policy and assess the impact of skills initiatives.

Table 3 shows the percentage of staff not fully proficient as recorded in successive skills surveys. This is usually called the 'skills gap' and relates to the number of currently employed staff, considered by

Figure 3
Percentage of people aged 19 to state pension age with no qualifications: by NUTS1 region

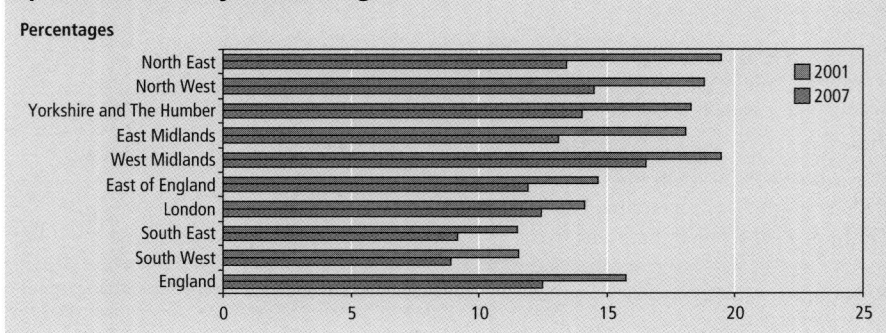

Source: Labour Force Survey, Office for National Statistics

Table 3
Percentage of staff considered to be not fully proficient: by NUTS1 region

	2003[1]	2004[1]	2005[1]	2007
North East	8.7	5.6	5.5	6.3
North West	10.1	6.4	5.8	5.3
Yorkshire and The Humber	12.7	9.1	7.5	4.8
East Midlands	10.2	7.8	6.2	6.8
West Midlands	11.7	8.3	4.8	5.4
East of England	11.0	6.5	5.2	7.8
London	9.5	5.4	5.8	6.7
South East	10.8	8.0	6.6	5.8
South West	10.0	7.8	5.1	6.2
England	10.5	7.1	5.9	6.1

Note:

1 SSC weights have been used; percentages for earlier years may differ from those included in reports published at the time.

Source: National Employers Skill Surveys, LSC research tool on www.researchtools.lsc.gov.uk

employers to be not fully proficient at their jobs. In 2003, NESS estimated that 2.3m employees throughout England were not fully proficient at their job; this equated to more than one in ten of those in employment. By 2007 the number of staff not fully proficient was estimated to have fallen by about one million to around one in sixteen (roughly 6 per cent). In 2007, differences between regions were not large, ranging from 4.8 per cent in Yorkshire and The Humber to 7.8 per cent in the East of England. It is important to remember that the skills required in each region are different and reflect the industry mix of the area; also the level of proficiency deemed necessary will vary from employer to employer. The expectation of employers, their perception of skills and recent employment history also influences responses to the survey.

Over the four year period between 2003 and 2007, Yorkshire and The Humber showed the greatest improvement in staff proficiency with more than a 60 per cent reduction in the number of employees (163,000 people), considered to be not fully proficient. The East of England showed the least reduction with 26 per cent. These estimates will not reflect changes to the skills required over time, nor the impact of staff turnover.

NESS also gives information on vacancies that are considered by employers to be hard to fill due to skill shortages, for example, a lack of applicants with the required skills. These types of vacancies can be a useful indicator of how training and up-skilling of the workforce is progressing. However, it must be remembered that skills required in each region may be different and it is the employers' perception of the skills required to do a particular job that feeds into information on skills gaps, and which

vacancies are hard to fill because of skill shortages.

In 2007 approximately 20 per cent of all vacancies in England were considered, by employers, to be 'hard to fill' due to skill shortages – categorised as skill shortage vacancies (SSVs). SSVs tend to measure skills issues external to a business, whereas skills gap information focuses on skill levels of the existing workforce within a business. London was estimated to have the highest rate of SSVs, at 26.1 per cent in 2007, followed by the South East with 22.5 per cent; the West Midlands region was at the lower end of the range with 15.5 per cent. Although more than half of the people between 19 and pension age in the South East, the South West and London were qualified to at least NVQ level 3 (Table 2) by 2007, these regions each had over 20 per cent of their vacancies considered 'hard to fill' due to skill shortages.

In order to assess the future capabilities of the labour force, the percentage of pupils achieving five or more grades A* to C at GCSE level or equivalent in each English region can be used as an indicator. Regional comparisons based on preliminary results for 2007/08 are shown in **Figure 5**. Each region is compared to the England average

Figure 4
Percentage of vacancies considered 'hard to fill'[1] due to skills shortages: by NUTS1 region, 2007

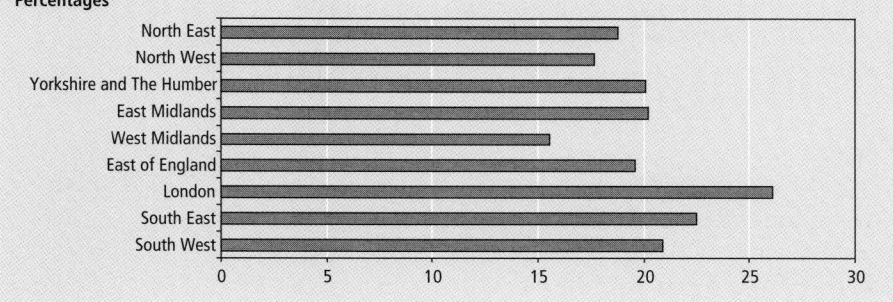

Note:
Source: National Employers Skills Survey

1 Vacancies are considered 'hard to fill' if there are a low number of applicants with the required skills, a lack of work experience the company demands or a lack of qualifications the company demands.

Figure 5
Pupils achieving five or more grades A* to C at GCSE level or equivalent: by NUTS1 region, 2007/08[1]

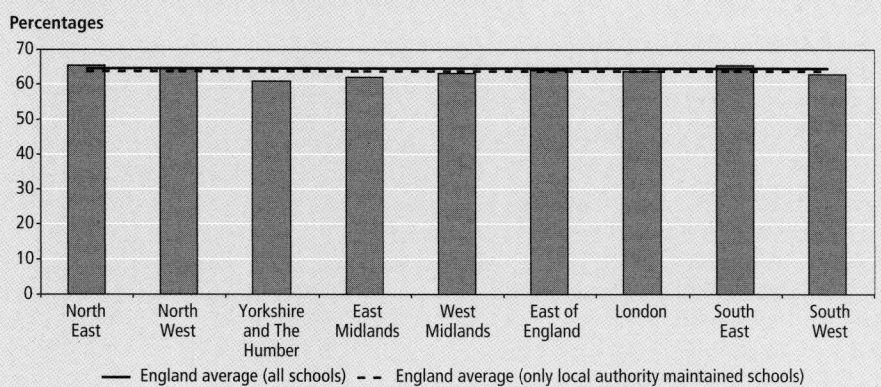

Note:
Source: Department for Children, Schools and Families

1 Provisional data, includes attempts and achievements by these pupils in previous academic years.

of 63.7 per cent; this average only takes local authority maintained schools into account. A second average can be calculated when taking into account information on the devolved administrations, which is based on all schools. This yields an average of 64.6 per cent for England. The average is higher when calculated on all schools, implying that pupils in non-local authority establishments achieve higher results.

Within local authority maintained schools in English regions, the South East, the East of England, London, the North East and the North West performed above the England average, while Yorkshire and The Humber, the East Midlands, the West Midlands and the South West performed below the England average. When taking into account all schools, English regions, except the South East, North East and North West, performed below the average of 64.6 per cent.

The proportion of pupils attaining five or more GCSEs at grades A* to C has increased in all regions. Since 2000/01 there has been an increase of 13.7 percentage points in the number of pupils achieving this standard throughout England. The largest increase has been in the North East, where proportions have increased from 43.9 per cent in 2000/01 to provisionally 65.5 per cent in 2007/08.

Recent focus on literacy and numeracy has led to a new measure being published, of five or more GCSEs grade A* to C which include English and Mathematics. Provisional data for 2007/08 indicate that the proportion of pupils achieving five or more GCSEs A* to C including English and Mathematics are between 14 (in the South West, London and the East of England) and 21 (in the North East) percentage points lower than the proportion of pupils gaining five A* to C passes in any subjects.

Figure 6 investigates the percentage differences from the England average for pupils gaining five A* to C passes in (a) any subjects and (b) subjects including English and Mathematics. Regional differences are less pronounced when any five subjects are included in the analysis. Regional differences range from 2.7 and 1.6 percentage points below the England average for Yorkshire and The Humber and the East Midlands, respectively, to the North East and South East each with 1.8 percentage points above the England average. If the five subjects include both English and Mathematics, the proportion of pupils in the North East and the North West achieving five A* to C grades falls below the national average. The opposite is true for the South West which moves from below the national average to 1.1 percentage points above.

Regional overview

Key figures on a regional basis indicate that:

- in 2006, London was the region with the highest GVA per hour worked, 22.9 percentage points above the UK average. Northern Ireland had the lowest GVA per hour worked (indexed to UK = 100), 16.1 percentage points below the UK average.

- London and the South East had the highest levels of gross disposable household income (GDHI) per head in 2006, at £16,939 and £15,367, respectively, while the North East (£11,846), Northern Ireland (£12,041) and Wales (£12,312) had the lowest GDHI per head.

- in the second quarter of 2008 the North East and the East of England had the strongest increases in export values to the EU, at 16.4 and 11.5 per cent, respectively, compared to 12 months earlier. Scotland, the East Midlands and the West Midlands experienced declines in their exports to the EU over the same period.

- the South East had the highest employment rate in the second quarter of 2008, at 79.4 per cent; Northern Ireland had the lowest rate, at 70.1 per cent, compared with the UK employment rate of 74.7 per cent.

Headline indicators

In order to gain an overview of the economic performance of the UK regions, this article investigates a selection of economic indicators. Currently, the most widely used indicator of regional economic performance is gross value added (GVA) per head, which is, among others, used as an indicator in regional policy decisions and the allocation of EU Structural Funds.

However, GVA per head does not give any indication of either regional productivity or the welfare of the residents of a region. GVA per head gives an indication of economic activity per head of population. To measure productivity, GVA per filled job and GVA per hour worked should be used, while gross disposable household income (GDHI) per head can be used to determine the welfare of residents of the UK regions.

Regional performance

Table 4 shows the regional economic performance in terms of GVA per head for 2000, 2002, 2004 and 2006 and indicates the average annual growth over the period 2000 to 2006. In terms of GVA per head London

---

Figure 6
Proportions of pupils achieving five or more A* to C GCSEs relative to England: by NUTS1 region, 2007/08

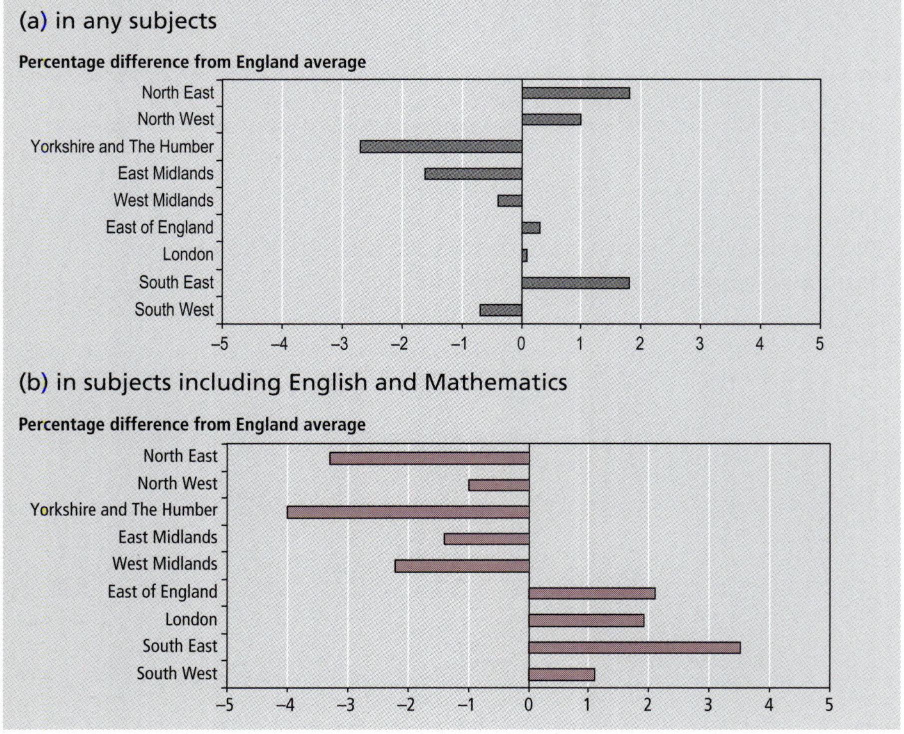

(a) in any subjects

Percentage difference from England average

(b) in subjects including English and Mathematics

Percentage difference from England average

Source: Department for Children, Schools and Families

Table 4
Headline workplace-based gross value added per head and average annual growth: by NUTS1 region

£ and percentages

	United Kingdom[1]	North East	North West	Yorkshire and The Humber	East Midlands	West Midlands	East of England	London	South East	South West	Wales	Scotland	Northern Ireland
2000	14,006	11,108	12,445	12,309	12,811	12,864	13,307	21,372	15,218	12,999	10,973	13,270	11,415
2002	15,462	12,221	13,667	13,555	14,150	13,996	14,701	23,652	16,901	14,439	12,074	14,578	12,474
2004	17,234	13,791	15,109	14,973	15,789	15,355	16,494	26,641	18,804	16,175	13,352	16,253	13,993
2006[2]	18,631	15,177	16,234	15,968	16,982	16,583	17,652	28,959	20,316	17,467	14,396	17,789	15,175
GVA per head average annual percentage growth, 2000–2006[2]	4.9	5.3	4.5	4.4	4.8	4.3	4.8	5.2	4.9	5.0	4.6	5.0	4.9

Notes:

1 UK less Extra-regio.
2 Provisional.

Source: Regional Accounts, Office for National Statistics

had by far the highest figure, at £28,959 in 2006, followed by the South East and the East of England (at £20,316 and £17,652, respectively). Wales, Northern Ireland and the North East had the lowest figures in 2006, far below the UK average. The average annual growth figures show that the North East, as one of the bottom GVA per head performer, and London, as the best performer, each had the highest growth rates, above five per cent. This was followed by the South West, Scotland, the South East and Northern Ireland.

Labour productivity

As workplace-based GVA per head does not take into account commuting effects, different labour market structures or age profiles, it is likely that this measure over- or under- states the actual economic performance of regions in terms of productivity and welfare. GVA per filled job and GVA per hour worked provide the most effective labour productivity indicators and help to compare regional performances in terms of productivity. While GVA per head looks at the entire regional workplace-based population and GVA per filled job looks at regional workforce jobs and therefore takes into account commuting effects and differing regional age profiles, GVA per hour worked additionally considers variations in labour market structures across regions, such as the proportions of full- and part-time workers or job share availability. Due to these reasons GVA per hour worked is the preferred indicator of productivity.

Figure 7 compares estimates for GVA per head, GVA per filled job and GVA per hour worked for 2006. It can be seen that GVA per hour worked generally exhibits fewer and smaller differences in regional economic performance when compared with the other two indicators. Like the GVA per head estimates in Table 4, London and the South East also had the highest productivity indicators, above the UK average.

Nevertheless, the productivity performance of London is much closer to the UK average than the region's GVA per head. This can be attributed to the strong inward commuting into London, which inflates its GVA per head measure as the number of people contributing to GVA increases, but the resident population remains unchanged. Two of the regions with the lowest GVA per head, Wales and the North East, performed much closer to the UK average in terms of GVA per hour worked. This is mainly due

to outward commuting and below average economic activity in these regions.

Figure 8 shows the regional GVA per hour worked productivity index on a time series basis. While in terms of average annual GVA per head growth the strongest growing regions were the North East and London, in terms of GVA per hour worked there was greater improvement in London, the South East and the East Midlands. Those regions that had the greatest deterioration were Wales, Northern

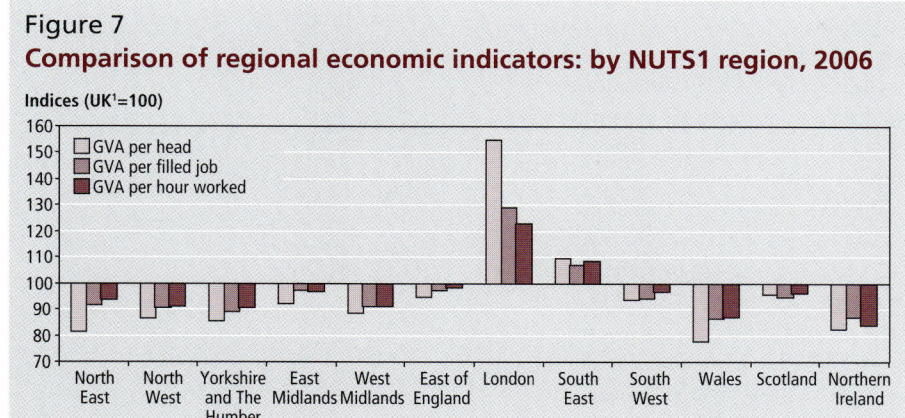

Figure 7
Comparison of regional economic indicators: by NUTS1 region, 2006

Indices (UK[1]=100)

- GVA per head
- GVA per filled job
- GVA per hour worked

Note:

1 UK less Extra-regio and statistical discrepancy.

Source: Office for National Statistics

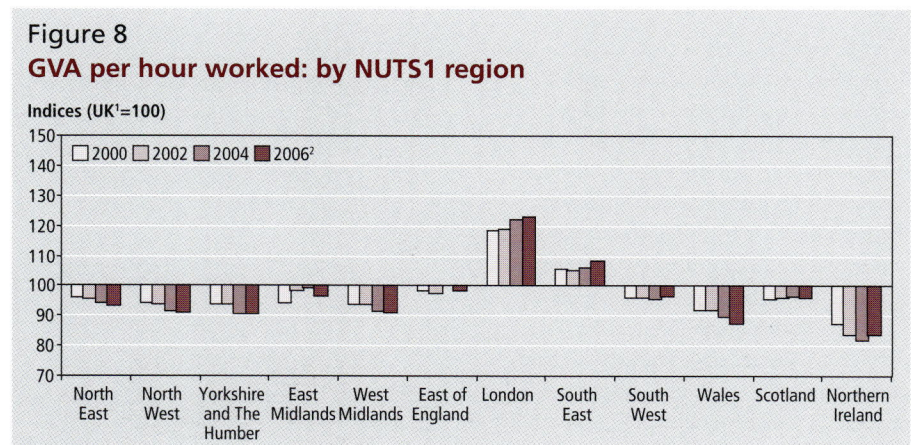

Figure 8
GVA per hour worked: by NUTS1 region

Indices (UK[1]=100)

- 2000
- 2002
- 2004
- 2006[2]

Notes:

1 UK less Extra-regio and statistical discrepancy.
2 Provisional.

Source: Office for National Statistics

Ireland, Yorkshire and The Humber and the North West. Generally, Figure 8 suggests that, since 2000, regional productivity differences between the highest and the lowest performing regions have widened. Productivity in London was the highest in all years and by 2006 was above the UK average by an additional 4.5 percentage points compared with 2000. The opposite occurred in Wales, where GVA per hour worked in 2006 was a further 4.7 percentage points below the UK average compared with 2000. The lowest productivity was experienced in Northern Ireland.

Welfare

The welfare of the residents of a region is another important indicator that helps understand differences in regional economic performances. Gross disposable household income (GDHI) by region gives an indication of regional welfare. By investigating GDHI per head, a residence-based measure, the analysis takes account of the population distribution both within and across regions and provides reliable comparisons of regional income levels. New GDHI estimates up to 2006 were published in May 2008 and are available at www.statistics.gov.uk/statbase/Product. asp?vlnk=14651. GDHI estimates are published at current basic prices and so do not take inflation effects or regional price differences into account.

Figure 9 shows GDHI per head estimates from 2000 to 2006, indexed to the UK average GDHI per head. London, the South East and the East of England were the only three regions where households had incomes above the UK average. While seven regions experienced convergence to the UK average, the remaining five regions had constant household incomes with respect to the UK average, implying that their GDHI per head grew at the same rate as the UK average over the period from 2000 to 2006. Those regions that were below the UK average and experienced convergence had a faster increasing GDHI per head than the UK average while the South East and the East of England saw their household incomes increase less than the UK average.

Comparing these outcomes with the regional productivity performance shown in Figure 8, it can be seen that, unlike GDHI per head, GVA per hour worked has been diverging from the UK average in most regions. Moreover, in terms of productivity some regions have been performing close to the average while their GDHI per head shows much stronger divergences.

The North East for example had a close to average but declining productivity performance since 2000 and at the same time the lowest but slightly increasing GDHI per head. One reason for the low GDHI per head might be the region's low employment and high unemployment rate (see Tables 6 and 7).

Gross median weekly earnings represent another indicator for regional welfare. **Figure 10** shows the gross median weekly pay for all full-time employees and its gender components, female and male full-time employees, in each region in 2007. London was the region with the highest gross median weekly pay in 2007, at £580.90, followed by the South East, at £480.70. These were the only regions above the UK average of £456.70. Northern Ireland (£401.90), the North East (£402.90) and Wales (£404.70) experienced the lowest earnings in 2007. The figure shows a clear gap between the gross median weekly pay for male and female full-time employees

in every region. In Northern Ireland the discrepancy was smallest. The weekly pay for male full-time employees was above the UK average in nine of the 12 NUTS1 regions, while the weekly pay of female full-time employees was only above the UK average in London and substantially below it in all other regions.

Other drivers of productivity

The focus section of this article has already covered skills – one of the productivity drivers identified by HM Treasury and the Department for Business, Enterprise & Regulatory Reform (BERR). Alongside skills, innovation, enterprise, competition and investment have been identified as productivity drivers and can help explain differences in productivity across regions. Due to quality concerns regarding the regional allocations of investment (net capital expenditure), this variable is currently not included in this article.

It is important to realise that alongside the drivers identified by HM Treasury

Figure 9
Headline gross disposable household income per head: by NUTS1 region

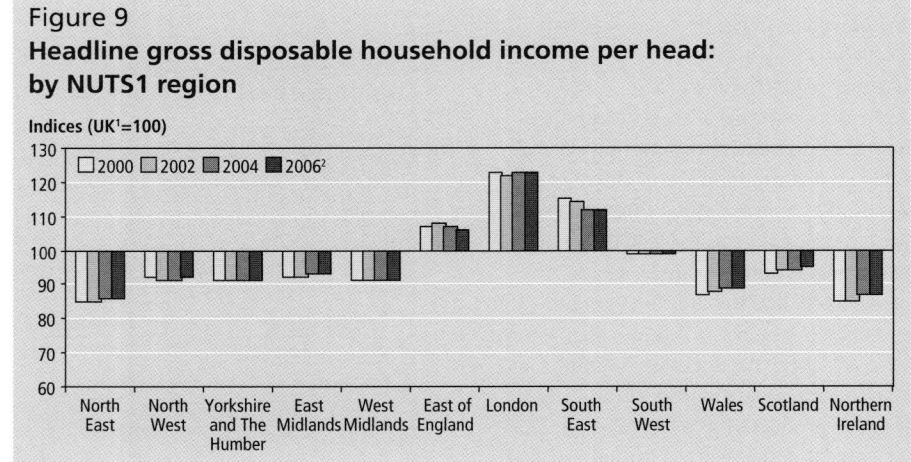

Indices (UK[1]=100)

Notes:
1 UK less Extra-regio.
2 Provisional.

Source: Regional Accounts, Office for National Statistics

Figure 10
Gross median weekly pay of full-time employees: by NUTS1 region, 2007

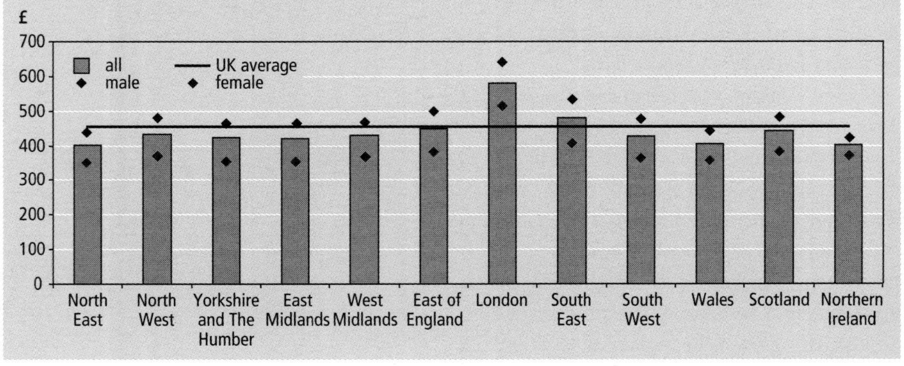

Source: Annual Survey of Hours and Earnings, Office for National Statistics

and BERR, other factors, such as economic participation, agglomeration and connectivity, industrial structure and region-specific assets have a strong influence on regional productivity performance.

This article uses expenditure on Research and Development (R&D) by businesses as a measure of innovation; the net change of VAT registrations and de-registrations serves as a measure of enterprise; and UK regional trade in goods is used as a measure of competition.

Innovation

Innovation is a necessary, although not sufficient, condition for economic success and is therefore recognised as an important driver of productivity. Innovation comprises, among others, the development of new technologies that increase efficiency and the introduction of new, more valuable goods and services. It also includes intangibles such as new methods of working and improvements to services.

R&D represents one of the determinants to the innovation process and is defined by the OECD in its Frascati Manual, which proposes a standard practice for surveys on R&D, as 'creative work undertaken on a systematic basis in order to increase the stock of knowledge, including knowledge of man, culture and society, and the use of this stock of knowledge to create new applications'. The OECD definition of R&D covers basic research, applied research and experimental development:

- basic research: experimental and theoretical work to obtain new knowledge of the underlying foundation of phenomena and observable facts, without any particular application or use in view
- applied research: work undertaken to acquire new knowledge, which is directed primarily towards a specific practical aim
- experimental development: systematic work, drawing on existing knowledge, which is directed at producing new materials, products or devices, installing new processes, systems and services, or at improving substantially those already produced or installed

The OECD definition excludes education, training and any other related scientific, technological, industrial, administrative or supporting activities.

Statistics on Business Expenditure on Research and Development (BERD),

consistent with these internationally agreed standards, are published annually (most recently in November 2007) and provide estimates of business expenditure on R&D for NUTS1 regions up to 2006. New estimates, up to 2007, will be published in the February REI article.

Figure 11 presents expenditure on R&D performed in UK businesses by region in 2000 and 2006. It also shows the regional average annual percentage growth over this period. The East of England and the South East had the highest business expenditure on R&D in 2000 and 2006, each with expenditures above £3 billion in 2006, thus making up the largest percentage share of total expenditure in the UK. Northern Ireland, Wales and the North East remained the regions with the lowest R&D expenditure since 2000 (below £300 million each). The regional average annual percentage growth rates show that those regions with low expenditure on R&D experienced the highest average annual growth rates between 2000 and 2006. Northern Ireland was the only region that

had one of the lowest expenditures on R&D and at the same time the lowest average annual growth rate. Those regions with high expenditures on R&D had relatively low average annual growth rates.

While Figure 11 has looked at absolute regional expenditures on R&D, **Figure 12** investigates R&D as a percentage of GVA, a measure commonly used in international comparisons as it takes account of the size of regional economies. The figure shows that since 2000 the East of England has been the region with by far the highest share of R&D expenditure in terms of GVA, with 3.6 per cent in 2006. The South East had the second highest share (1.9 per cent), which however has been declining since 2000, when the share of expenditure on R&D was 2.4 per cent. This was followed by R&D expenditure in the North West and the South West with shares of 1.5 per cent each in 2006. London, Yorkshire and The Humber, Wales and Northern Ireland had the lowest shares in 2006 at around 0.5 per cent each. London's very low share of expenditure on R&D may not be suggestive

Figure 11
Expenditure on R&D performed in UK businesses: by NUTS1 region

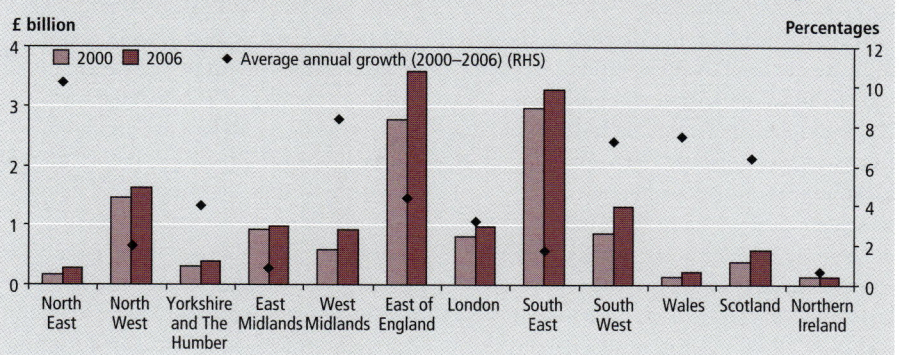

Source: Statistics on Business Expenditure on Research and Development, Office for National Statistics

Figure 12
Business expenditure on R&D as a percentage of workplace-based GVA: by NUTS1 region

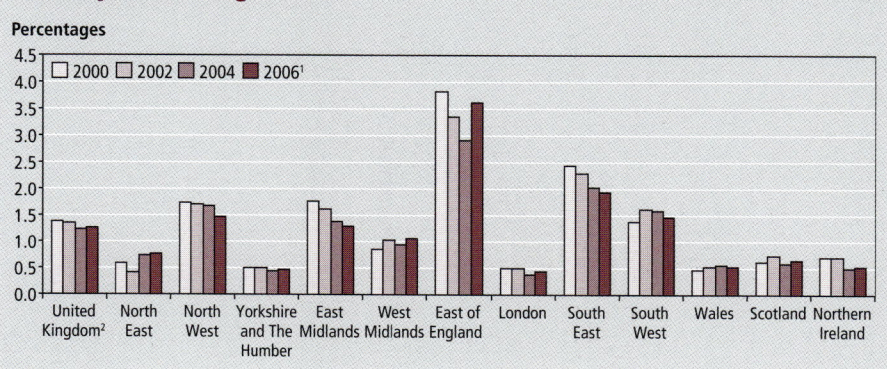

Notes:
1 Provisional.
2 UK less Extra-regio and statistical discrepancy.

Source: Office for National Statistics

of low levels of innovation but could reflect how regional industry composition affects R&D as an indicator of innovation. London has a large concentration of service industries, but service industries may not be R&D intensive (within the OECD definition) if, for example, they rely heavily on human capital. If innovation occurs in other forms it may not be captured by the R&D measure.

Enterprise

Enterprise is another driver of productivity as it stands for the presence of a positive entrepreneurial culture; for the ease of starting-up and overcoming the barriers to enterprise; for a sustainable stock of enterprise activity in an economy; and the ability of firms to grow. In order to investigate the pattern of business start-ups and closures VAT registrations and de-registrations as published by BERR are the best official indicator to use. New data on business start-ups for 2007 will be released in November 2008 and will be included in the February edition of this article. This more comprehensive series which has been developed includes PAYE as well as VAT-registered businesses.

VAT registrations and de-registrations indicate the level of entrepreneurship and the health of the business population. Among the many factors that influence the pattern of business start-ups, the most important is economic growth, which encourages new ventures and creates demand for business. **Figure 13** shows the net changes in VAT-registered businesses for all UK regions between 2000 and 2006. The figure also depicts the average annual percentage growth rate over this period.

The bars in Figure 13 show that all NUTS1 regions had positive net changes in VAT registrations and de-registrations from 2000 to 2006. This implies that over this time period more enterprises were registered than de-registered in the UK regions. Furthermore, the figure shows that all regions, except Northern Ireland, experienced positive average annual growth in their net change from 2000 to 2006.

In 2006, the lowest net changes in VAT registrations were in Northern Ireland (575), the North East (1,155) and Wales (1,305). However, two of these regions – the North East and Wales – experienced relatively high average annual growth rates, implying that their net changes have been increasing, due to a higher number of VAT registrations and fewer de-registrations. The highest average annual growth rates were experienced in Scotland and the North West. The highest net change in VAT registrations and de-registrations in 2006 was in London and the South East, with 7,250 and 6,015, respectively. However, in terms of average annual growth, these two regions experienced among the lowest growth rates.

Interestingly, all regions, except the North West, that had net changes in VAT registrations and de-registrations above 3,000 are situated next to each other (London, the East of England, the East Midlands, the South East and the South West).

When investigating the absolute numbers of registrations and de-registrations, respectively, it can be seen that regions with high registration rates tend to also have high de-registrations rates. This is partly due to the difference in the sizes of regions. The regions with the largest populations (the South East, London, the North West

and the East of England) also had the largest registrations and de-registration rates and, as seen in Figure 13, the highest net changes. However, the fact that high registration rates are often associated with high de-registration rates can also be due to the effects of market sorting (when more competitive entrants push the less productive ones out of a market) being more significant in some regions than others. Another reason could be the industrial mix in each region, with some sectors prone to higher rates of turnover than others.

Competition

Vigorous competition enhances productivity by creating incentives to innovate and it ensures that resources are allocated to the most efficient firms. It also forces existing firms to organise work more effectively through imitations of organisational structures and technology. It is however important to take into account that exports do not cover all aspects of competition in a region.

HM Revenue & Customs (HMRC) publishes statistics on regional trade in goods to the European Union (EU) and non-EU destinations by statistical value. Trade in goods by definition excludes intangibles and services. The statistical value of export trade is calculated as the value of the goods plus the cost of movement to the country's border.

Table 5 presents the latest estimates that go up to the second quarter of 2008. The total value of UK exports to all destinations for the twelve months ending June 2008 increased by 8.1 per cent compared with the twelve months ending June 2007.

As the EU is the main export destination for UK goods, the table separates exports to EU and non-EU destinations. In terms of exports to the EU, the value of UK exports for the twelve months ending June 2008 increased by 6.8 per cent compared with the twelve months ending June 2007. This increase was driven by increased exports to the EU by nine UK regions, of which the North East and the East of England had the strongest increases, at 16.4 and 11.5 per cent, respectively. Scotland, the East Midlands and the West Midlands were the only three regions that experienced declines in their exports to the EU over this 12 months period, at 11.7, 6.8 and 2.3 per cent declines, respectively.

In terms of the latest quarter estimates (2008 Q2) compared with the previous quarter, all regions except the East

Figure 13
Net change[1] in VAT registrations and de-registrations: by NUTS1 region

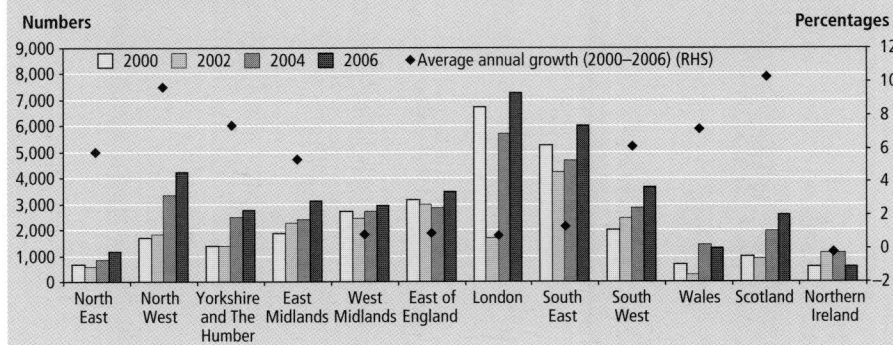

Note: Source: Department for Business, Enterprise & Regulatory Reform

1 Net change is the net gain or loss in the stock of registered enterprises each year, equal to registrations less de-registrations.

Table 5

UK regional trade in goods – statistical value of exports: by NUTS1 region

£ million

	United Kingdom	North East	North West	Yorkshire and The Humber	East Midlands	West Midlands	East of England	London	South East	South West	Wales	Scotland	Northern Ireland
EU[1] exports													
2006 Q3	31,854	1,285	3,063	1,580	2,483	2,677	2,647	2,181	4,295	1,587	1,368	1,709	804
2006 Q4	31,086	1,398	2,566	1,694	2,152	2,171	2,793	2,164	4,708	1,641	1,307	1,694	835
2007 Q1	31,747	1,303	2,794	1,765	2,296	2,267	3,164	2,244	4,598	1,725	1,440	1,569	847
2007 Q2	31,263	1,287	2,952	1,696	2,036	2,325	2,998	2,066	4,609	1,580	1,415	1,635	850
12 months ending June 2007	125,950	5,273	11,375	6,735	8,967	9,440	11,602	8,655	18,210	6,533	5,530	6,607	3,336
2007 Q3	30,662	1,330	2,773	1,649	2,038	2,033	2,914	2,183	4,490	1,633	1,313	1,378	830
2007 Q4	32,951	1,557	2,854	1,725	2,058	2,314	3,196	2,152	4,891	1,725	1,331	1,527	855
2008 Q1[2]	34,644	1,648	3,119	1,741	2,177	2,395	3,291	2,287	4,899	1,799	1,517	1,473	872
2008 Q2[2]	36,229	1,605	3,244	1,853	2,086	2,478	3,532	2,362	5,214	1,906	1,654	1,456	964
12 months ending June 2008	134,486	6,140	11,990	6,968	8,359	9,220	12,933	8,984	19,494	7,063	5,815	5,834	3,521
Non-EU exports													
2006 Q3	21,910	713	2,301	1,254	1,742	1,534	1,826	3,137	3,655	1,074	981	1,624	460
2006 Q4	23,575	848	2,421	1,313	1,791	1,579	2,022	3,939	3,531	1,113	947	1,495	505
2007 Q1	21,183	807	2,261	1,247	1,622	1,479	1,775	3,477	3,112	917	839	1,683	469
2007 Q2	23,968	1,009	2,484	1,564	1,655	1,607	2,004	3,448	4,003	992	957	1,991	521
12 months ending June 2007	90,636	3,377	9,467	5,378	6,810	6,199	7,627	14,001	14,301	4,096	3,724	6,793	1,955
2007 Q3	23,007	1,021	2,417	1,402	1,685	1,595	1,843	3,402	3,667	1,100	851	2,012	520
2007 Q4	25,138	1,261	2,462	1,762	1,784	1,801	2,001	3,595	4,125	1,155	912	1,894	578
2008 Q1[2]	23,827	1,164	2,452	1,641	1,743	1,767	2,167	3,195	3,893	1,052	869	1,834	555
2008 Q2[2]	27,720	1,335	2,862	1,712	1,940	1,990	2,508	3,661	4,993	1,182	1,074	2,066	638
12 months ending June 2008	99,692	4,781	10,193	6,517	7,152	7,153	8,519	13,853	16,678	4,489	3,706	7,806	2,291

Notes:

Source: UK Regional Trade in Goods Statistics, HM Revenue & Customs

1 EU data refer to EU25 up to 2006 Q4 and EU27 from 2007 Q1.
2 Provisional.

Midlands, the North East and Scotland experienced an increase in the value of their exports to the EU. Northern Ireland and Wales had the strongest increase, at 10.6 and 9.0 per cent, respectively.

UK exports to non-EU destinations for the twelve months ending June 2008 increased even stronger than exports to the EU compared with the twelve months ending June 2007. The total value of UK exports to non-EU destinations increased by 10.0 per cent, with the strongest increases in the North East (41.6 per cent), Northern Ireland (17.2 per cent), the South East (16.6 per cent) and the West Midlands (15.4 per cent). Only two regions – London and Wales – experienced slight declines in their exports to non-EU destinations.

Concerning last quarter estimates (2008 Q2) for export values to non-EU destinations, all regions experienced an increase. The South East and Wales saw the largest increases (at 28.3 and 23.6 per cent, respectively). The smallest increase was experienced by Yorkshire and The Humber, with 4.3 per cent growth from the previous quarter.

Figure 14 shows all main destinations of UK regional exports in 2007. Exports to the 27 countries that are part of the European Union (EU 27) made up the

biggest percentage, above 50 per cent of exports, in all regions except in London and Scotland. The second main destination for UK exports was North America. London and Wales exported over 20 per cent of their exports to North America, while the South West exported only 12.9 per cent to this destination. Asia and Oceania presents the third most popular export destination. London, the East Midlands, and Yorkshire and The Humber exported around 15 per cent

of their exports to Asia and Oceania, while Wales and Northern Ireland only exported 7.2 per cent each of their exports to this destination.

In order to take into account the differing sizes of regional economies instead of only investigating the absolute numbers of export value, as has been shown in Table 5, **Figure 15** shows the value of export goods as a percentage of workplace-based regional GVA from 2000 to 2006. In 2006, exports from the East Midlands accounted

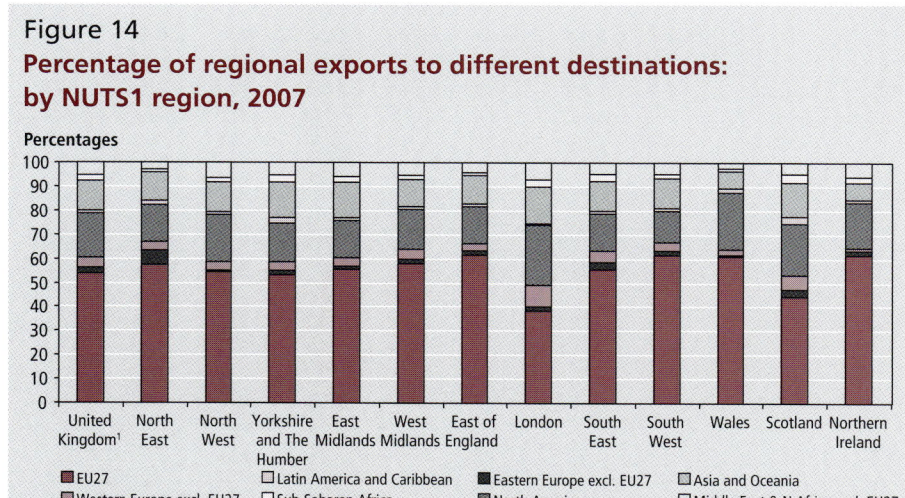

Figure 14

Percentage of regional exports to different destinations: by NUTS1 region, 2007

Percentages

Note: Source: HM Revenue & Customs, Regional Trade Statistics
1 The UK value excludes low value, unknown and suppressed trade.

Figure 15
Value of total export goods as a percentage of workplace-based GVA: by NUTS1 region

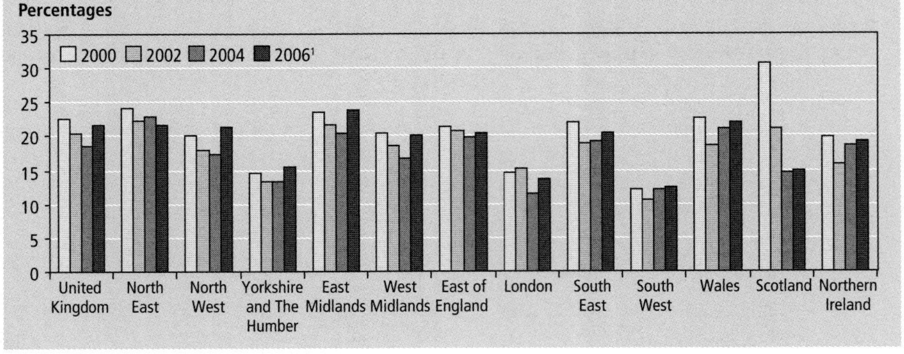

Percentages

Note:

1 Provisional.

Source: HM Revenue & Customs, Regional Trade Statistics and Office for National Statistics

for the highest percentage of GVA (at 23.9 per cent), 2.3 percentage points above the UK average. The region, where exports accounted for the smallest percentage of GVA in 2006 was the South West, with 12.2 per cent. In terms of this indicator's development over time, from 2000 to 2004 the UK average value of export goods as a percentage of GVA has been declining while it has been increasing from 2004 to 2006. Most regions show the same trend. Scotland, however, experienced a significant drop from 2000 to 2006, with exports in 2006 accounting for 15.9 percentage points less in terms of GVA than in 2000.

The labour market

Table 6 shows the seasonally adjusted employment rate, the number of people of working-age in employment, expressed as a proportion of the population, from the Labour Force Survey (LFS).

In quarter two (April to June) of 2008, the UK employment rate was 74.7 per cent, up 0.2 percentage points from the previous year and down 0.1 percentage points from quarter one (January to March) of 2008. Regional rates varied from 79.4 per cent in the South East to 70.1 per cent in Northern Ireland in the second quarter.

Six regions had an increase in the employment rate over the year. London had a rise of 1.8 percentage points and the rate for the South East increased by 0.9 percentage points. Six regions experienced falls in the employment rate. The North East had an annual fall of 1.2 percentage points, Northern Ireland and Scotland both had an annual fall of 0.5 percentage points.

Table 7 shows the unemployment rate (according to the internationally-consistent International Labour Organisation definition) for people aged 16 and over from the LFS. The UK rate in the second quarter of 2008 was 5.4 per cent, unchanged from a year ago but up 0.2 percentage points on the previous quarter. Regionally, the rates ranged from 7.5 per cent in the North East to 3.8 per cent in the South West.

Over the year, the unemployment rate had decreased in seven regions. The unemployment in Wales decreased by 0.6 percentage points and in London by 0.5 percentage points. The unemployment rate rose in five regions. The North East had an increase of 1.2 percentage points while the East Midlands showed a rise of 0.7 percentage points.

Table 8 shows economic inactivity rates for people of working-age from the LFS. The UK rate in the second quarter of 2008 was 20.9 per cent, unchanged from the previous quarter and down 0.3 percentage points on a year earlier. Across the regions, rates varied from 17.1 per cent in the South East to 26.8 per cent in Northern Ireland.

Compared with a year earlier, six regions had a decrease in their inactivity rates, and thus a corresponding increase in their working-age activity rates. London had the largest annual fall of 1.5 percentage points. Four regions had an increase in the economic inactivity rate over the year. The largest annual rise was in Scotland with 0.9 percentage points.

Table 9 shows the number of employee jobs, not seasonally adjusted, from the Employer Surveys. The number of UK

Table 6
Employment[1] rates for people of working-age: by NUTS1 region

Percentages, seasonally adjusted

		United Kingdom	North East	North West	Yorkshire and The Humber	East Midlands	West Midlands	East of England	London	South East	South West	England	Wales	Scotland	Northern Ireland
2005	Apr–Jun	74.7	70.3	73.2	74.3	76.6	74.5	78.8	69.4	78.9	78.9	75.1	71.4	75.0	68.4
	Jul–Sep	74.8	69.7	73.6	74.6	77.2	74.0	78.6	69.7	78.8	78.4	75.1	72.2	75.3	70.1
	Oct–Dec	74.4	70.1	72.8	74.2	77.2	73.4	77.6	69.4	78.7	77.7	74.6	71.9	75.3	69.0
2006	Jan–Mar	74.7	71.3	73.5	74.4	77.0	73.9	77.3	69.9	78.9	78.3	75.0	71.6	75.1	69.4
	Apr–Jun	74.6	71.6	73.2	74.2	77.0	73.9	77.0	69.7	78.9	78.6	74.9	71.3	74.7	69.9
	Jul–Sep	74.6	71.0	73.6	73.5	77.0	73.9	77.2	69.8	78.8	77.9	74.8	72.0	75.5	69.3
	Oct–Dec	74.5	70.9	72.8	73.7	76.5	73.0	77.0	70.0	78.7	78.2	74.6	71.8	76.2	69.9
2007	Jan–Mar	74.3	71.0	72.5	72.8	75.9	72.5	77.3	70.1	78.2	78.0	74.4	71.7	76.6	70.6
	Apr–Jun	74.5	71.4	72.6	73.3	76.0	72.7	77.4	69.7	78.5	78.1	74.5	72.1	77.0	70.6
	Jul–Sep	74.6	72.1	72.4	73.4	75.7	73.0	77.2	70.7	78.8	78.6	74.7	71.3	76.6	70.1
	Oct–Dec	74.8	71.6	72.8	73.7	75.8	73.3	78.1	70.4	78.9	79.3	75.0	71.6	76.6	69.9
2008	Jan–Mar	74.8	70.2	72.4	74.0	76.2	73.2	77.7	71.1	79.5	79.0	75.0	72.0	76.5	69.7
	Apr–Jun	74.7	70.2	72.2	73.4	75.7	72.5	77.7	71.5	79.4	78.8	74.8	72.6	76.5	70.1

Note:

1 Includes employees, self-employed, participants on government-supported training schemes and unpaid family workers.

Source: Labour Force Survey, Office for National Statistics

Table 7
Unemployment rates for people aged 16 and over: by NUTS1 region

Percentages, seasonally adjusted

		United Kingdom	North East	North West	Yorkshire and The Humber	East Midlands	West Midlands	East of England	London	South East	South West	England	Wales	Scotland	Northern Ireland
2005	Apr–Jun	4.8	6.8	4.4	4.8	4.3	4.6	3.9	7.1	3.8	3.2	4.7	4.5	5.5	5.0
	Jul–Sep	4.8	6.6	4.4	4.6	4.4	4.7	4.0	6.7	4.0	3.6	4.7	4.7	5.5	4.3
	Oct–Dec	5.2	6.6	5.0	5.5	4.5	5.3	4.6	7.3	4.2	4.0	5.2	5.0	5.2	4.5
2006	Jan–Mar	5.2	6.5	4.9	5.4	5.0	5.3	4.9	7.6	4.5	3.6	5.3	4.8	5.3	4.3
	Apr–Jun	5.5	6.1	5.3	5.8	5.5	5.6	5.0	7.8	4.7	3.8	5.5	5.6	5.5	4.3
	Jul–Sep	5.5	6.7	5.5	6.0	5.3	6.1	4.8	7.8	4.5	3.8	5.6	5.4	5.0	4.7
	Oct–Dec	5.5	6.7	5.4	6.0	5.7	6.7	4.5	7.7	4.3	3.9	5.6	5.3	5.2	4.2
2007	Jan–Mar	5.5	6.8	5.8	6.3	5.5	6.5	4.8	7.1	4.7	4.0	5.6	5.6	4.9	4.1
	Apr–Jun	5.4	6.3	5.8	5.5	5.0	6.7	4.6	7.4	4.3	4.0	5.5	5.5	4.7	3.8
	Jul–Sep	5.3	6.1	6.0	5.4	5.7	6.4	5.1	6.1	4.5	4.0	5.4	5.3	4.8	3.8
	Oct–Dec	5.2	5.8	5.9	5.3	5.2	5.8	4.4	6.6	4.5	3.7	5.2	5.1	4.9	4.2
2008	Jan–Mar	5.2	6.5	6.0	5.0	5.5	6.2	4.5	6.9	3.9	3.7	5.3	5.4	4.6	4.6
	Apr–Jun	5.4	7.5	6.3	6.1	5.7	6.3	4.6	6.9	4.2	3.8	5.6	4.9	4.2	4.2

Source: Labour Force Survey, Office for National Statistics

Table 8
Economic inactivity rates for people of working-age: by NUTS1 region

Percentages, seasonally adjusted

		United Kingdom	North East	North West	Yorkshire and The Humber	East Midlands	West Midlands	East of England	London	South East	South West	England	Wales	Scotland	Northern Ireland
2005	Apr–Jun	21.5	24.5	23.3	21.8	19.9	21.8	18.0	25.2	17.9	18.4	21.1	25.2	20.6	27.9
	Jul–Sep	21.4	25.3	22.9	21.7	19.2	22.2	18.0	25.2	17.8	18.6	21.1	24.2	20.3	26.7
	Oct–Dec	21.4	24.9	23.3	21.4	19.0	22.3	18.6	25.0	17.7	19.0	21.2	24.3	20.5	27.6
2006	Jan–Mar	21.1	23.7	22.7	21.3	18.8	21.9	18.6	24.2	17.4	18.7	20.7	24.7	20.6	27.5
	Apr–Jun	21.0	23.6	22.6	21.2	18.4	21.5	18.8	24.3	17.1	18.3	20.6	24.3	20.9	26.9
	Jul–Sep	21.0	23.9	22.0	21.7	18.6	21.2	18.8	24.1	17.5	18.9	20.7	23.8	20.5	27.2
	Oct–Dec	21.1	23.9	22.9	21.5	18.7	21.6	19.1	24.0	17.7	18.5	20.8	24.0	19.6	27.0
2007	Jan–Mar	21.2	23.7	22.9	22.2	19.6	22.3	18.6	24.4	17.9	18.6	21.1	23.9	19.4	26.3
	Apr–Jun	21.2	23.8	22.7	22.3	20.0	21.8	18.8	24.6	17.8	18.5	21.1	23.5	19.1	26.6
	Jul–Sep	21.1	23.1	22.9	22.4	19.6	21.8	18.5	24.6	17.4	18.0	20.9	24.5	19.4	27.0
	Oct–Dec	21.0	23.9	22.5	22.0	19.9	22.1	18.2	24.4	17.2	17.6	20.8	24.5	19.4	27.0
2008	Jan–Mar	20.9	24.8	22.8	22.0	19.2	21.7	18.5	23.5	17.1	17.9	20.7	23.8	19.6	26.9
	Apr–Jun	20.9	24.0	22.7	21.7	19.5	22.4	18.5	23.1	17.1	18.0	20.6	23.5	20.0	26.8

Source: Labour Force Survey, Office for National Statistics

Table 9
Employee jobs:[1] by NUTS1 region

Thousands, not seasonally adjusted

	United Kingdom	North East	North West	Yorkshire and The Humber	East Midlands	West Midlands	East of England	London	South East	South West	England	Wales	Scotland	Northern Ireland
Jun 04	26,383	1,003	2,982	2,211	1,762	2,305	2,301	3,915	3,617	2,145	22,242	1,133	2,296	682
Jun 05	26,771	1,039	2,996	2,212	1,814	2,329	2,306	3,969	3,663	2,197	22,524	1,160	2,358	696
Jun 06	26,953	1,047	2,976	2,211	1,831	2,348	2,349	3,988	3,679	2,218	22,646	1,187	2,379	706
Jun 07	27,068	1,050	3,002	2,238	1,841	2,371	2,360	4,018	3,657	2,208	22,744	1,192	2,377	719
Sep 07	27,128	1,053	3,002	2,237	1,859	2,375	2,373	4,027	3,664	2,222	22,813	1,195	2,380	720
Dec 07[2]	27,144	1,068	3,027	2,246	1,862	2,388	2,394	4,076	3,702	2,231	22,994	1,188	2,399	721
Mar 08	27,192	1,057	2,980	2,230	1,847	2,374	2,380	4,050	3,678	2,210	22,806	1,175	2,378	722
Jun 08	27,214	1,059	2,987	2,236	1,849	2,380	2,394	4,064	3,701	2,228	22,897	1,179	2,385	722

Source: Employer Surveys

Notes:

1   Employee jobs figures are of a measure of jobs rather than people. For example, if a person holds two jobs, each job will be counted in the employee jobs total. Employees jobs figures come from quarterly surveys of employers carried out by ONS and administrative sources.

2   Revised.

employee jobs in June 2008 was 27.2 million, which marks an increase of 146 thousand over the year since June 2007. In percentage terms, this was a 0.5 per cent increase.

There were annual increases in nine regions. The largest percentage rise was in the East of England (1.5 per cent).

Table 10 shows the claimant count rate (referring to people claiming Jobseeker's Allowance benefits as a proportion of the workforce). The UK rate was 2.9 per cent in September 2008, up 0.1 percentage point from August 2008, and up 0.3 percentage points on a year earlier. This national rate masks large variations between regions and component countries of the UK. For September 2008, the North East had the highest claimant count rate in the UK at 4.6 per cent. The North East was followed by the West Midlands (3.9 per cent), the North West and Yorkshire and The Humber (3.5 per cent each). The lowest claimant counts were measured in the South West and South East (1.8 per cent each). The claimant count rate was 3.0 per cent in Scotland, and 3.3 per cent in Wales and Northern Ireland.

London was the only region not to have an increase in the claimant count rate compared with a year ago. The largest increases were in the North East (0.7 percentage points), Northern Ireland (0.6 percentage points), Yorkshire and

The Humber and Wales (each with 0.5 percentage points). The rate in London was unchanged.

CONTACT

 elmr@ons.gsi.gov.uk

REFERENCES

Department for Business, Enterprise & Regulatory Reform (2007) *Business Start-Ups and Closures: VAT Registrations and De-registrations in 2006* at stats.berr.gov.uk/ed/vat/index.htm

Department for Business, Enterprise & Regulatory Reform *Three-Year Survival Rates of VAT-Registered Businesses by Region* at stats.berr.gov.uk/ed/survival/

Department for Children, Schools and Families (2008) *GCSE and Equivalent Examination Results in England 2006/07 (Revised)* Statistical First Release at www.dfes.gov.uk/rsgateway/DB/SFR/s000768/index.shtml

Department for Innovation, Universities and Skills (2008) *The Level of Highest Qualification Held by Adults: England 2007* Statistical First Release at www.dfes.gov.uk/rsgateway/DB/SFR/s000777/index.shtml

Department for Innovation, Universities and Skills (2006) *Leitch Report* at www.dcsf.gov.uk/furthereducation/uploads/documents/2006-12%20LeitchReview1.pdf

Department for Education and Skills (2003) *21st Century Skills: Realising Our Potential National Skills Strategy* at www.dcsf.gov.uk/skillsstrategy/index.cfm?fuseaction=content.view&CategoryID=6

Department for Education and Skills *Skills Strategy* at www.dcsf.gov.uk/skillsstrategy/

HM Revenue & Customs (2007) *UK Regional Trade Statistics* at www.uktradeinfo.com/index.cfm?task=td_regstats_press

HM Treasury (2004) *Productivity in the UK 5: Benchmarking UK Productivity Performance. A Consultation on Productivity Indicators* at www.hm-treasury.gov.uk/4971.htm

Learning and Skills Council *National Employers Skills Survey* at research.lsc.gov.uk/LSC+Research/published/ness/

Office for National Statistics *Annual Survey of Hours and Earnings* at www.statistics.gov.uk/statbase/product.asp?vlnk=13101

Table 10
Claimant count rates:[1] by NUTS1 region

Percentages, seasonally adjusted

		United Kingdom	North East	North West	Yorkshire and The Humber	East Midlands	West Midlands	East of England	London	South East	South West	England	Wales	Scotland	Northern Ireland
2003		3.0	4.5	3.2	3.3	2.8	3.5	2.1	3.6	1.7	1.9	2.9	3.3	3.7	4.1
2004		2.7	4.0	2.8	2.8	2.5	3.3	2.0	3.5	1.6	1.6	2.6	3.0	3.4	3.6
2005		2.7	3.9	2.9	2.9	2.5	3.4	2.1	3.4	1.6	1.6	2.6	3.0	3.2	3.3
2006		2.9	4.1	3.3	3.3	2.8	3.9	2.3	3.4	1.8	1.8	2.9	3.1	3.1	3.2
2007		2.7	4.0	3.1	3.0	2.6	3.7	2.1	3.0	1.6	1.6	2.6	2.8	2.8	2.8
2007	Sep	2.6	3.9	3.1	3.0	2.6	3.6	2.0	2.9	1.5	1.5	2.6	2.8	2.7	2.7
	Oct	2.6	3.9	3.1	2.9	2.5	3.6	2.0	2.8	1.5	1.5	2.5	2.7	2.6	2.7
	Nov	2.5	3.9	3.0	2.9	2.5	3.5	2.0	2.8	1.5	1.4	2.5	2.7	2.6	2.7
	Dec	2.5	3.8	3.0	2.9	2.4	3.5	1.9	2.8	1.5	1.4	2.5	2.7	2.6	2.7
2008	Jan	2.5	3.8	3.0	2.8	2.4	3.4	1.9	2.7	1.5	1.4	2.4	2.7	2.5	2.7
	Feb	2.5	3.9	3.0	2.9	2.4	3.4	1.9	2.7	1.5	1.4	2.4	2.7	2.5	2.8
	Mar	2.5	3.9	3.0	2.9	2.4	3.4	1.9	2.7	1.5	1.4	2.4	2.7	2.5	2.8
	Apr	2.5	3.9	3.1	2.9	2.5	3.4	1.9	2.7	1.5	1.4	2.5	2.8	2.5	2.8
	May	2.6	4.0	3.1	3.0	2.5	3.5	2.0	2.7	1.5	1.5	2.5	2.8	2.6	2.9
	Jun	2.6	4.1	3.2	3.1	2.6	3.6	2.0	2.7	1.6	1.5	2.6	2.9	2.7	3.0
	Jul	2.7	4.2	3.3	3.2	2.7	3.7	2.1	2.8	1.6	1.6	2.7	3.0	2.7	3.1
	Aug	2.8	4.4	3.4	3.3	2.8	3.8	2.2	2.9	1.7	1.7	2.8	3.2	2.9	3.2
	Sep	2.9	4.6	3.5	3.5	2.9	3.9	2.3	2.9	1.8	1.8	2.9	3.3	3.0	3.3

Note:

Source: Jobcentre Plus administrative system

1 Count of claimants of Jobseeker's Allowance expressed as a percentage of the total workforce – that is, workforce jobs plus claimants.

Office for National Statistics *Business Expenditure on Research & Development by Government Office Region* at www.statistics.gov.uk/statbase/tsdataset. asp?vlnk=572

Office for National Statistics *Introduction of Automatic Occupation Coding in ASHE* at www.statistics.gov.uk/cci/article.asp?id=1843

Office for National Statistics *Regional Household Income March 2007* Statistical First Release at www.statistics.gov.uk/statbase/product. asp?vlnk=14651

Office for National Statistics *Regional Snapshot: Education and Training, Notes and Definitions* at www.statistics.gov.uk/statbase/Product. asp?vlnk=14712

Office for National Statistics (2008) *Regional Trends 40* at www.statistics.gov.uk/RegionalTrends40/

Office for National Statistics (2008) 'Regional Economic Indicators February 2008 with a focus on regional productivity' *Economic & Labour Market Review* 2(2), pp 48–61 and at www.statistics.gov.uk/elmr/02_08/

Office for National Statistics (2007) 'Regional Economic Indicators February 2007 with a focus on the differences in regional economic performance' *Economic & Labour Market Review* 1(2), pp 52-64 and at www.statistics.gov.uk/elmr/02_07/

Office for National Statistics (2007) 'Regional Productivity' *The ONS Productivity Handbook: A Statistical Overview and Guide*, Chapter 11, pp 147–156 and at www.statistics.gov.uk/about/data/guides/ productivity/ch11.asp

Organisation for Economic Co-operation and Development (2002) *Frascati Manual: Proposed Standard Practice for Surveys on Research and Experimental Development*

Organisation for Economic Co-operation and Development (2003) 'Identifying the Determinants of Regional Performances' *Working Party on Territorial Indicators*

TECHNICAL NOTE

Sampling variability

Some of the estimates used in this article are based on sample surveys and are therefore subject to sampling variability. The table below shows sampling variabilities for the Labour Force Survey as it relates to Table 1.

These sampling variability ranges represent '95 per cent confidence intervals'. This means that in 95 per cent of samples the range is expected to contain the true value.

Confidence intervals around estimates of working-age population[1] by highest qualification:[2] by NUTS1 region, second quarter 2008

Percentages

	Degree or equivalent	Higher education qualifications below degree	GCE A level or equivalent & apprenticeships	GCSE grades A* to C or equivalent	Other qualifications	No qualifications
United Kingdom	± 0.3	± 0.2	± 0.3	± 0.3	± 0.3	± 0.3
North East	± 1.4	± 0.9	± 1.6	± 1.6	± 1.2	± 1.3
North West	± 1.0	± 0.7	± 1.0	± 1.0	± 0.7	± 0.9
Yorkshire and The Humber	± 1.1	± 0.7	± 1.2	± 1.1	± 1.0	± 1.0
East Midlands	± 1.1	± 0.8	± 1.2	± 1.2	± 1.1	± 1.0
West Midlands	± 1.1	± 0.7	± 1.2	± 1.2	± 0.9	± 1.1
East of England	± 1.1	± 0.7	± 1.1	± 1.1	± 0.9	± 0.9
London	± 1.2	± 0.6	± 0.9	± 0.9	± 1.1	± 0.8
South East	± 1.0	± 0.6	± 0.9	± 0.9	± 0.8	± 0.7
South West	± 1.2	± 0.8	± 1.2	± 1.2	± 0.9	± 0.8
England	± 0.4	± 0.2	± 0.4	± 0.4	± 0.3	± 0.3
Wales	± 1.5	± 1.0	± 1.5	± 1.6	± 1.1	± 1.3
Scotland	± 1.1	± 0.9	± 1.2	± 1.0	± 0.8	± 0.9
Northern Ireland	± 1.7	± 1.0	± 1.7	± 1.6	± 0.9	± 1.6

Notes: *Source: Labour Force Survey, Office for National Statistics*

1   Males aged 16 to 64 and females aged 16 to 59.
2   For summary of qualifications and equivalents, see www.statistics.gov.uk/statbase/Product.asp?vlnk=14712

Key time series

1 National accounts aggregates

Last updated: 24/10/08

Seasonally adjusted

	£ million		Indices (2003 = 100)						
	At current prices		Value indices at current prices		Chained volume indices			Implied deflators[3]	
	Gross domestic product (GDP) at market prices	Gross value added (GVA) at basic prices	GDP at market prices[1]	GVA at basic prices	Gross national disposable income at market prices[2]	GDP at market prices	GVA at basic prices	GDP at market prices	GVA at basic prices
	YBHA	ABML	YBEU	YBEX	YBFP	YBEZ	CGCE	YBGB	CGBV
2002	1,075,564	957,094	94.4	94.3	97.1	97.3	97.2	97.0	97.0
2003	1,139,746	1,015,008	100.0	100.0	100.0	100.0	100.0	100.0	100.0
2004	1,200,595	1,068,574	105.3	105.3	102.8	102.8	102.7	102.5	102.5
2005	1,252,505	1,115,121	109.9	109.9	104.2	104.9	104.9	104.8	104.7
2006	1,321,860	1,177,232	116.0	116.0	106.1	107.8	107.9	107.5	107.5
2007	1,401,042	1,247,721	122.9	122.9	109.6	111.1	111.1	110.6	110.6
2002 Q1	263,968	234,651	92.6	92.5	96.1	96.5	96.5	96.0	95.8
2002 Q2	267,473	238,071	93.9	93.8	96.2	96.9	96.8	96.9	96.9
2002 Q3	270,655	240,922	95.0	94.9	98.2	97.5	97.5	97.4	97.4
2002 Q4	273,468	243,450	96.0	95.9	98.1	98.1	98.1	97.8	97.8
2003 Q1	278,207	247,866	97.6	97.7	99.4	98.7	98.7	98.9	98.9
2003 Q2	283,305	252,613	99.4	99.6	99.2	99.6	99.6	99.8	99.9
2003 Q3	287,130	255,626	100.8	100.7	99.8	100.4	100.3	100.4	100.4
2003 Q4	291,104	258,903	102.2	102.0	101.6	101.3	101.3	100.8	100.7
2004 Q1	293,234	260,813	102.9	102.8	101.8	101.8	101.7	101.1	101.1
2004 Q2	299,120	266,134	105.0	104.9	102.5	102.7	102.7	102.2	102.1
2004 Q3	301,608	268,390	105.9	105.8	102.2	102.9	102.9	102.8	102.8
2004 Q4	306,633	273,237	107.6	107.7	104.5	103.6	103.6	103.9	103.9
2005 Q1	308,895	274,979	108.4	108.4	104.2	104.0	104.0	104.2	104.2
2005 Q2	313,126	278,928	109.9	109.9	105.6	104.7	104.7	105.0	104.9
2005 Q3	313,026	278,181	109.9	109.6	103.3	105.1	105.1	104.5	104.3
2005 Q4	317,458	283,033	111.4	111.5	103.9	105.6	105.7	105.5	105.5
2006 Q1	324,523	289,466	113.9	114.1	105.2	106.8	106.9	106.6	106.7
2006 Q2	326,609	290,681	114.6	114.6	106.1	107.6	107.7	106.6	106.4
2006 Q3	332,954	296,264	116.9	116.8	106.4	108.0	108.1	108.2	108.0
2006 Q4	337,774	300,821	118.5	118.5	106.9	109.0	109.0	108.8	108.7
2007 Q1	342,597	304,405	120.2	120.0	107.5	109.9	110.0	109.4	109.1
2007 Q2	348,439	310,094	122.3	122.2	108.9	110.8	110.8	110.4	110.3
2007 Q3	353,386	314,835	124.0	124.1	109.6	111.6	111.7	111.1	111.1
2007 Q4	356,620	318,387	125.2	125.5	112.5	112.2	112.2	111.6	111.9
2008 Q1	362,212	323,349	127.1	127.4	113.6	112.5	112.5	113.0	113.3
2008 Q2	363,719	324,403	127.6	127.8	111.9	112.5	112.5	113.5	113.6
2008 Q3						111.9	112.0		

Percentage change, quarter on corresponding quarter of previous year

			IHYO	ABML[4]	YBGO[4]	IHYR	ABMM[4]	IHYU	ABML/ABMM[4]
2002 Q1	4.4	4.5	4.4	4.5	2.9	1.8	1.4	2.5	3.1
2002 Q2	5.1	5.5	5.1	5.5	2.7	2.0	1.5	3.1	3.8
2002 Q3	5.9	6.0	5.9	6.0	3.9	2.2	1.9	3.6	4.1
2002 Q4	5.7	5.8	5.7	5.8	4.1	2.4	2.4	3.2	3.3
2003 Q1	5.4	5.6	5.4	5.6	3.5	2.3	2.3	3.0	3.3
2003 Q2	5.9	6.1	5.9	6.1	3.1	2.8	2.9	3.0	3.1
2003 Q3	6.1	6.1	6.1	6.1	1.7	2.9	2.9	3.1	3.1
2003 Q4	6.4	6.3	6.4	6.3	3.6	3.2	3.3	3.1	3.0
2004 Q1	5.4	5.2	5.4	5.2	2.5	3.1	3.0	2.2	2.2
2004 Q2	5.6	5.4	5.6	5.4	3.4	3.1	3.1	2.4	2.2
2004 Q3	5.0	5.0	5.0	5.0	2.4	2.5	2.6	2.4	2.4
2004 Q4	5.3	5.5	5.3	5.5	2.9	2.3	2.3	3.0	3.2
2005 Q1	5.3	5.4	5.3	5.4	2.3	2.2	2.3	3.0	3.1
2005 Q2	4.7	4.8	4.7	4.8	3.0	1.9	2.0	2.7	2.7
2005 Q3	3.8	3.6	3.8	3.6	1.1	2.1	2.2	1.6	1.4
2005 Q4	3.5	3.6	3.5	3.6	-0.6	2.0	2.0	1.5	1.5
2006 Q1	5.1	5.3	5.1	5.3	1.0	2.7	2.8	2.3	2.4
2006 Q2	4.3	4.2	4.3	4.2	0.5	2.7	2.8	1.5	1.4
2006 Q3	6.4	6.5	6.4	6.5	3.0	2.8	2.8	3.5	3.6
2006 Q4	6.4	6.3	6.4	6.3	2.9	3.2	3.1	3.1	3.0
2007 Q1	5.6	5.2	5.6	5.2	2.2	2.9	2.8	2.6	2.3
2007 Q2	6.7	6.7	6.7	6.7	2.7	3.0	2.9	3.6	3.7
2007 Q3	6.1	6.3	6.1	6.3	2.9	3.3	3.3	2.7	2.9
2007 Q4	5.6	5.8	5.6	5.8	5.2	2.9	2.9	2.6	2.9
2008 Q1	5.7	6.2	5.7	6.2	5.7	2.3	2.3	3.3	3.8
2008 Q2	4.4	4.6	4.4	4.6	2.7	1.5	1.6	2.8	3.0
2008 Q3						0.3	0.3		

Source: Office for National Statistics

Notes:

1 "Money GDP".
2 This series is only updated once a quarter, in line with the full quarterly national accounts data set.
3 Based on chained volume measures and current price estimates of expenditure components of GDP.
4 Derived from these identification (CDID) codes.

2 Gross domestic product: by category of expenditure

Last updated: 24/10/08

£ million, chained volume measures, reference year 2003, seasonally adjusted

	Domestic expenditure on goods and services at market prices											
	Final consumption expenditure			Gross capital formation								
	Households	Non-profit institutions[1]	General government	Gross fixed capital formation	Changes in inventories[2]	Acquisitions less disposals of valuables	Total	Exports of goods and services	Gross final expenditure	less imports of goods and services	Statistical discrepancy (expenditure)	Gross domestic at product market prices
	ABJR	HAYO	NMRY	NPQT	CAFU	NPJR	YBIM	IKBK	ABMG	IKBL	GIXS	ABMI
2002	693,124	27,576	224,973	184,701	2,289	183	1,133,077	285,433	1,418,531	309,982	0	1,108,508
2003	714,608	27,668	232,819	186,700	3,983	−37	1,165,741	290,677	1,456,418	316,672	0	1,139,746
2004	736,857	27,198	240,672	195,782	4,371	−42	1,204,838	304,699	1,509,537	338,359	0	1,171,178
2005	751,288	27,212	244,850	200,187	4,814	−354	1,227,997	329,491	1,557,487	362,211	0	1,195,276
2006	766,378	28,289	248,776	212,146	4,575	290	1,260,454	365,818	1,626,272	397,076	0	1,229,196
2007	789,163	29,269	253,200	227,188	6,849	535	1,306,204	349,290	1,655,493	389,724	628	1,266,397
2002 Q1	171,546	6,871	55,781	44,562	1,372	66	280,217	70,659	350,877	76,009	0	274,918
2002 Q2	172,790	6,867	56,313	45,610	367	48	282,005	72,740	354,783	78,682	0	276,010
2002 Q3	173,839	6,907	56,455	46,422	287	62	284,033	72,259	356,315	78,344	0	277,923
2002 Q4	174,949	6,931	56,424	48,107	263	7	286,822	69,775	356,556	76,947	0	279,657
2003 Q1	176,080	6,949	57,130	46,805	−647	−8	286,469	73,942	360,416	79,207	0	281,208
2003 Q2	178,451	6,889	57,711	46,131	190	94	289,609	71,934	361,538	77,711	0	283,851
2003 Q3	179,545	6,913	58,472	45,964	2,065	−68	292,894	71,671	364,561	78,577	0	285,990
2003 Q4	180,532	6,917	59,506	47,800	2,375	−55	296,769	73,130	369,903	81,177	0	288,697
2004 Q1	182,394	6,950	60,023	48,869	−684	112	297,664	74,062	371,726	81,742	0	289,984
2004 Q2	184,099	6,823	59,806	49,385	603	−90	299,726	75,645	376,270	83,564	0	292,706
2004 Q3	184,893	6,760	60,210	49,061	936	−96	301,763	76,739	378,502	85,230	0	293,272
2004 Q4	185,471	6,665	60,633	48,467	3,516	32	304,786	78,253	383,039	87,823	0	295,216
2005 Q1	186,342	6,867	60,787	48,845	3,151	−158	305,833	77,173	383,006	86,553	0	296,453
2005 Q2	187,191	6,806	61,208	49,264	1,895	86	306,448	80,809	387,257	88,955	0	298,302
2005 Q3	188,172	6,784	61,370	51,286	187	−201	307,597	84,033	391,629	92,100	0	299,529
2005 Q4	189,583	6,755	61,485	50,792	−419	−81	308,119	87,476	395,595	94,603	0	300,992
2006 Q1	189,581	6,945	61,989	50,715	1,593	101	310,924	96,005	406,929	102,518	0	304,412
2006 Q2	192,015	7,037	61,854	52,139	−153	229	313,121	98,339	411,460	105,003	0	306,456
2006 Q3	191,988	7,120	62,329	53,681	1,844	−28	316,934	85,722	402,656	94,804	0	307,853
2006 Q4	192,794	7,187	62,604	55,611	1,291	−12	319,475	85,752	405,227	94,751	0	310,475
2007 Q1	194,532	7,243	62,927	56,457	1,449	73	322,682	86,055	408,737	95,628	122	313,232
2007 Q2	196,339	7,260	63,193	56,209	623	329	323,953	86,847	410,800	95,360	151	315,591
2007 Q3	198,538	7,314	63,468	56,764	2,744	44	328,872	88,508	417,380	99,549	173	318,004
2007 Q4	199,754	7,452	63,612	57,758	2,033	89	330,697	87,880	418,576	99,187	182	319,570
2008 Q1	201,446	7,602	64,227	56,609	485	205	330,573	88,535	419,108	98,860	203	320,452
2008 Q2	201,195	7,728	64,544	55,031	1,163	429	330,089	88,493	418,583	98,333	203	320,453
2008 Q3												318,851

Percentage change, quarter on corresponding quarter of previous year

2002 Q1	4.0	−1.4	4.0	0.9			3.3	−2.6	2.0	2.6		1.8
2002 Q2	4.1	−0.4	4.4	1.6			2.8	3.1	2.9	6.0		2.0
2002 Q3	3.4	0.6	3.3	3.1			2.8	4.5	3.2	6.5		2.2
2002 Q4	3.2	1.4	2.1	9.0			3.9	−0.8	2.9	4.5		2.4
2003 Q1	2.6	1.1	2.4	5.0			2.2	4.6	2.7	4.2		2.3
2003 Q2	3.3	0.3	2.5	1.1			2.7	−1.1	1.9	−1.2		2.8
2003 Q3	3.3	0.1	3.6	−1.0			3.1	−0.8	2.3	0.3		2.9
2003 Q4	3.2	−0.2	5.5	−0.6			3.5	4.8	3.7	5.5		3.2
2004 Q1	3.6	0.0	5.1	4.4			3.9	0.2	3.1	3.2		3.1
2004 Q2	3.2	−1.0	3.6	7.1			3.8	5.2	4.1	7.5		3.1
2004 Q3	3.0	−2.2	3.0	6.7			3.0	7.1	3.8	8.5		2.5
2004 Q4	2.7	−3.6	1.9	1.4			2.7	7.0	3.6	8.2		2.3
2005 Q1	2.2	−1.2	1.3	0.0			2.7	4.2	3.0	5.9		2.2
2005 Q2	1.7	−0.2	2.3	−0.2			1.9	6.8	2.9	6.5		1.9
2005 Q3	1.8	0.4	1.9	4.5			1.9	9.5	3.5	8.1		2.1
2005 Q4	2.2	1.4	1.4	4.8			1.1	11.8	3.3	7.7		2.0
2006 Q1	1.7	1.1	2.0	3.8			1.7	24.4	6.2	18.4		2.7
2006 Q2	2.6	3.4	1.1	5.8			2.2	21.7	6.2	18.0		2.7
2006 Q3	2.0	5.0	1.6	4.7			3.0	2.0	2.8	2.9		2.8
2006 Q4	1.7	6.4	1.8	9.5			3.7	−2.0	2.4	0.2		3.2
2007 Q1	2.6	4.3	1.5	11.3			3.8	−10.4	0.4	−6.7		2.9
2007 Q2	2.3	3.2	2.2	7.8			3.5	−11.7	−0.2	−9.2		3.0
2007 Q3	3.4	2.7	1.8	5.7			3.8	3.3	3.7	5.0		3.3
2007 Q4	3.6	3.7	1.6	3.9			3.5	2.5	3.3	4.7		2.9
2008 Q1	3.6	5.0	2.1	0.3			2.4	2.9	2.5	3.4		2.3
2008 Q2	2.5	6.4	2.1	−2.1			1.9	1.9	1.9	3.1		1.5
2008 Q3												0.3

Notes:

1 Non-profit institutions serving households (NPISH).
2 This series includes a quarterly alignment adjustment.

Source: Office for National Statistics

3 Labour market summary

Last updated: 15/10/08

United Kingdom (thousands), seasonally adjusted

All aged 16 and over

	All	Total economically active	Total in employment	Unemployed	Economically inactive	Economic activity rate (%)	Employment rate (%)	Unemployment rate (%)	Economic inactivity rate (%)
	1	2	3	4	5	6	7	8	9
All persons	MGSL	MGSF	MGRZ	MGSC	MGSI	MGWG	MGSR	MGSX	YBTC
Jun–Aug 2006	48,283	30,801	29,109	1,693	17,482	63.8	60.3	5.5	36.2
Jun–Aug 2007	48,686	30,866	29,220	1,646	17,820	63.4	60.0	5.3	36.6
Sep–Nov 2007	48,782	31,001	29,368	1,633	17,782	63.5	60.2	5.3	36.5
Dec–Feb 2008	48,879	31,108	29,494	1,614	17,770	63.6	60.3	5.2	36.4
Mar–May 2008	48,975	31,169	29,541	1,628	17,805	63.6	60.3	5.2	36.4
Jun–Aug 2008	49,073	31,211	29,419	1,792	17,862	63.6	60.0	5.7	36.4
Male	MGSM	MGSG	MGSA	MGSD	MGSJ	MGWH	MGSS	MGSY	YBTD
Jun–Aug 2006	23,447	16,665	15,692	973	6,782	71.1	66.9	5.8	28.9
Jun–Aug 2007	23,678	16,759	15,817	943	6,919	70.8	66.8	5.6	29.2
Sep–Nov 2007	23,733	16,826	15,894	931	6,908	70.9	67.0	5.5	29.1
Dec–Feb 2008	23,789	16,865	15,931	934	6,924	70.9	67.0	5.5	29.1
Mar–May 2008	23,844	16,902	15,953	949	6,942	70.9	66.9	5.6	29.1
Jun–Aug 2008	23,900	16,927	15,867	1,060	6,972	70.8	66.4	6.3	29.2
Female	MGSN	MGSH	MGSB	MGSE	MGSK	MGWI	MGST	MGSZ	YBTE
Jun–Aug 2006	24,836	14,136	13,416	720	10,700	56.9	54.0	5.1	43.1
Jun–Aug 2007	25,008	14,107	13,403	703	10,901	56.4	53.6	5.0	43.6
Sep–Nov 2007	25,049	14,175	13,474	701	10,874	56.6	53.8	4.9	43.4
Dec–Feb 2008	25,090	14,243	13,564	680	10,846	56.8	54.1	4.8	43.2
Mar–May 2008	25,131	14,267	13,588	679	10,864	56.8	54.1	4.8	43.2
Jun–Aug 2008	25,173	14,284	13,552	732	10,889	56.7	53.8	5.1	43.3

All aged 16 to 59/64

	All	Total economically active	Total in employment	Unemployed	Economically inactive	Economic activity rate (%)	Employment rate (%)	Unemployment rate (%)	Economic inactivity rate (%)
	10	11	12	13	14	15	16	17	18
All persons	YBTF	YBSK	YBSE	YBSH	YBSN	MGSO	MGSU	YBTI	YBTL
Jun–Aug 2006	37,382	29,607	27,939	1,668	7,776	79.2	74.7	5.6	20.8
Jun–Aug 2007	37,574	29,614	27,993	1,622	7,960	78.8	74.5	5.5	21.2
Sep–Nov 2007	37,617	29,722	28,111	1,612	7,894	79.0	74.7	5.4	21.0
Dec–Feb 2008	37,659	29,800	28,206	1,594	7,860	79.1	74.9	5.3	20.9
Mar–May 2008	37,702	29,833	28,229	1,604	7,869	79.1	74.9	5.4	20.9
Jun–Aug 2008	37,748	29,862	28,094	1,768	7,886	79.1	74.4	5.9	20.9
Male	YBTG	YBSL	YBSF	YBSI	YBSO	MGSP	MGSV	YBTJ	YBTM
Jun–Aug 2006	19,388	16,272	15,310	963	3,115	83.9	79.0	5.9	16.1
Jun–Aug 2007	19,558	16,333	15,401	933	3,225	83.5	78.7	5.7	16.5
Sep–Nov 2007	19,592	16,403	15,480	923	3,189	83.7	79.0	5.6	16.3
Dec–Feb 2008	19,627	16,426	15,501	924	3,201	83.7	79.0	5.6	16.3
Mar–May 2008	19,661	16,449	15,512	938	3,211	83.7	78.9	5.7	16.3
Jun–Aug 2008	19,694	16,475	15,426	1,048	3,220	83.7	78.3	6.4	16.3
Female	YBTH	YBSM	YBSG	YBSJ	YBSP	MGSQ	MGSW	YBTK	YBTN
Jun–Aug 2006	17,995	13,334	12,629	705	4,661	74.1	70.2	5.3	25.9
Jun–Aug 2007	18,016	13,281	12,592	689	4,735	73.7	69.9	5.2	26.3
Sep–Nov 2007	18,024	13,319	12,630	689	4,705	73.9	70.1	5.2	26.1
Dec–Feb 2008	18,033	13,374	12,705	670	4,659	74.2	70.5	5.0	25.8
Mar–May 2008	18,041	13,384	12,717	666	4,658	74.2	70.5	5.0	25.8
Jun–Aug 2008	18,053	13,387	12,668	719	4,666	74.2	70.2	5.4	25.8

Notes:

Relationship between columns: 1 = 2 + 5; 2 = 3 + 4; 6 = 2/1; 7 = 3/1; 8 = 4/2;
9 = 5/1; 10 = 11 + 14; 11 = 12 + 13; 15 = 11/10; 16 = 12/10; 17 = 13/11; 18 = 14/10
The Labour Force Survey is a survey of the population of private households,
student halls of residence and NHS accommodation.

Source: Labour Force Survey, Office for National Statistics
Labour Market Statistics Helpline: 01633 456901

4 Prices

Last updated: 14/10/08

Percentage change over 12 months

Not seasonally adjusted

	Consumer prices						Producer prices			
	Consumer prices index (CPI)			Retail prices index (RPI)			Output prices		Input prices	
	All items	CPI excluding indirect taxes (CPIY)[1]	CPI at constant tax rates (CPI-CT)	All items	All items excluding mortgage interest payments (RPIX)	All items excluding mortgage interest payments and indirect taxes (RPIY)[2]	All manufactured products	Excluding food, beverages, tobacco and petroleum products	Materials and fuels purchased by manufacturing industry	Excluding food, beverages, tobacco and petroleum products
	D7G7	EL2S	EAD6	CZBH	CDKQ	CBZX	PLLU[3]	PLLV[3,4]	RNNK[3,4]	RNNQ[3,4]
2004 Jan	1.4	1.5	1.3	2.6	2.4	2.0	0.7	0.1	−1.9	−1.6
2004 Feb	1.3	1.3	1.1	2.5	2.3	1.9	0.6	0.2	−3.5	−2.8
2004 Mar	1.1	1.1	1.0	2.6	2.1	1.7	0.3	0.2	−1.4	−2.2
2004 Apr	1.1	1.1	1.0	2.5	2.0	1.8	0.7	0.1	1.7	−1.0
2004 May	1.5	1.4	1.3	2.8	2.3	2.2	1.3	0.0	4.1	0.2
2004 Jun	1.6	1.5	1.4	3.0	2.3	2.3	1.4	0.1	2.1	0.0
2004 Jul	1.4	1.4	1.2	3.0	2.2	2.0	1.6	0.4	2.0	0.1
2004 Aug	1.3	1.3	1.1	3.2	2.2	2.0	1.7	0.8	3.3	1.3
2004 Sep	1.1	1.0	0.9	3.1	1.9	1.7	2.0	0.9	6.3	3.0
2004 Oct	1.2	1.2	1.1	3.3	2.1	2.0	2.5	1.3	7.5	3.9
2004 Nov	1.5	1.4	1.4	3.4	2.2	2.2	2.5	1.4	4.8	3.3
2004 Dec	1.7	1.7	1.6	3.5	2.5	2.5	1.8	0.8	2.7	2.8
2005 Jan	1.6	1.7	1.5	3.2	2.1	2.0	1.4	0.9	7.6	5.4
2005 Feb	1.7	1.7	1.6	3.2	2.1	2.0	1.6	0.9	9.0	6.3
2005 Mar	1.9	2.0	1.8	3.2	2.4	2.3	1.8	1.0	9.3	5.8
2005 Apr	1.9	2.0	1.9	3.2	2.3	2.3	2.3	1.1	8.6	5.4
2005 May	1.9	2.0	1.8	2.9	2.1	2.2	1.6	1.0	6.2	4.6
2005 Jun	2.0	2.2	1.9	2.9	2.2	2.2	1.5	0.8	10.6	5.9
2005 Jul	2.3	2.5	2.3	2.9	2.4	2.5	2.0	1.0	13.3	7.6
2005 Aug	2.4	2.6	2.3	2.8	2.3	2.3	2.1	0.9	12.1	6.7
2005 Sep	2.5	2.6	2.4	2.7	2.5	2.5	2.3	0.9	9.3	4.9
2005 Oct	2.3	2.5	2.3	2.5	2.4	2.3	1.8	0.5	8.2	5.6
2005 Nov	2.1	2.3	2.1	2.4	2.3	2.3	1.5	0.5	13.6	8.8
2005 Dec	1.9	2.1	1.8	2.2	2.0	2.0	1.9	1.1	18.0	11.4
2006 Jan	1.9	2.1	1.9	2.4	2.3	2.3	2.5	1.4	15.8	10.1
2006 Feb	2.0	2.1	2.0	2.4	2.3	2.3	2.3	1.4	15.2	10.1
2006 Mar	1.8	1.9	1.7	2.4	2.1	2.2	2.2	1.5	13.1	9.2
2006 Apr	2.0	2.1	2.0	2.6	2.4	2.3	2.3	1.9	15.6	9.8
2006 May	2.2	2.3	2.2	3.0	2.9	2.8	2.9	2.0	13.7	8.4
2006 Jun	2.5	2.6	2.4	3.3	3.1	3.2	3.1	2.5	11.3	8.1
2006 Jul	2.4	2.4	2.3	3.3	3.1	3.2	2.6	2.1	10.6	7.7
2006 Aug	2.5	2.6	2.4	3.4	3.3	3.4	2.3	1.7	8.4	6.7
2006 Sep	2.4	2.6	2.3	3.6	3.2	3.3	1.6	1.7	5.4	5.5
2006 Oct	2.4	2.7	2.3	3.7	3.2	3.3	1.3	2.0	3.9	4.5
2006 Nov	2.7	3.0	2.6	3.9	3.4	3.6	1.4	1.9	2.3	2.8
2006 Dec	3.0	3.2	2.9	4.4	3.8	3.9	1.7	1.6	1.7	1.5
2007 Jan	2.7	2.9	2.6	4.2	3.5	3.7	1.5	1.6	−3.4	−0.5
2007 Feb	2.8	2.9	2.6	4.6	3.7	3.9	1.9	2.0	−2.1	−0.2
2007 Mar	3.1	3.1	2.9	4.8	3.9	4.0	2.2	2.2	−0.3	1.0
2007 Apr	2.8	2.9	2.6	4.5	3.6	3.7	1.8	1.8	−1.5	0.0
2007 May	2.5	2.6	2.3	4.3	3.3	3.4	1.9	1.9	0.6	1.9
2007 Jun	2.4	2.5	2.2	4.4	3.3	3.3	1.9	1.7	1.7	2.2
2007 Jul	1.9	2.0	1.7	3.8	2.7	2.6	2.0	1.8	0.3	0.6
2007 Aug	1.8	1.9	1.6	4.1	2.7	2.6	2.1	2.0	−0.2	1.0
2007 Sep	1.8	1.7	1.6	3.9	2.8	2.8	2.6	1.9	6.0	3.6
2007 Oct	2.1	1.9	1.8	4.2	3.1	3.0	3.6	1.8	9.4	4.6
2007 Nov	2.1	1.9	1.8	4.3	3.2	3.0	4.5	1.9	12.1	5.6
2007 Dec	2.1	2.0	1.9	4.0	3.1	3.1	4.7	2.2	13.2	6.9
2008 Jan	2.2	2.1	2.0	4.1	3.4	3.3	5.7	3.0	20.4	11.0
2008 Feb	2.5	2.5	2.3	4.1	3.7	3.6	5.7	2.8	20.9	11.9
2008 Mar	2.5	2.6	2.3	3.8	3.5	3.6	6.2	2.9	20.8	12.7
2008 Apr	3.0	3.0	2.7	4.2	4.0	3.9	7.4	4.1	25.3	16.6
2008 May	3.3	3.3	3.1	4.3	4.4	4.4	9.1	5.6	30.2	18.9
2008 Jun	3.8	3.9	3.6	4.6	4.8	4.9	9.8	6.0	34.0	21.1
2008 Jul	4.4	4.5	4.2	5.0	5.3	5.4	10.0	6.3	31.4	21.4
2008 Aug	4.7	4.9	4.5	4.8	5.2	5.4	9.1	5.6	28.8	20.8
2008 Sep	5.2	5.4	5.0	5.0	5.5	5.6	8.5	5.4	24.5	20.0

Notes:

Source: Office for National Statistics

1   The taxes excluded are VAT, duties, insurance premium tax, air passenger duty and stamp duty on share transactions.
2   The taxes excluded are council tax, VAT, duties, vehicle excise duty, insurance premium tax and air passenger duty.
3   Derived from these identification (CDID) codes.
4   These derived series replace those previously shown.

NOTES TO TABLES

Identification (CDID) codes

The four-character identification code at the top of each alpha column of data is the ONS reference for that series of data on our time series database. Please quote the relevant code if you contact us about the data.

Conventions

Where figures have been rounded to the final digit, there may be an apparent slight discrepancy between the sum of the constituent items and the total shown. Although figures may be given in unrounded form to facilitate readers' calculation of percentage changes, rates of change, etc, this does not imply that the figures can be estimated to this degree of precision as they may be affected by sampling variability or imprecision in estimation methods.

The following standard symbols are used:

..	not available
-	nil or negligible
P	provisional
–	break in series
R	revised
r	series revised from indicated entry onwards

CONCEPTS AND DEFINITIONS

Labour Force Survey 'monthly' estimates

Labour Force Survey (LFS) results are three-monthly averages, so consecutive months' results overlap. Comparing estimates for overlapping three-month periods can produce more volatile results, which can be difficult to interpret.

Labour market summary

Economically active

People aged 16 and over who are either in employment or unemployed.

Economically inactive

People who are neither in employment nor unemployed. This includes those who want a job but have not been seeking work in the last four weeks, those who want a job and are seeking work but not available to start work, and those who do not want a job.

Employment and jobs

There are two ways of looking at employment: the number of people with jobs, or the number of jobs. The two concepts are not the same as one person can have more than one job. The number of people with jobs is measured by the Labour Force Survey (LFS) and includes people aged 16 or over who do paid work (as an employee or self-employed), those who have a job that they are temporarily away from, those on government-supported training and employment programmes, and those doing unpaid family work. The number of jobs is measured by workforce jobs and is the sum of employee jobs (as measured by surveys of employers), self-employment jobs from the LFS, people in HM Forces, and government-supported trainees. Vacant jobs are not included.

Unemployment

The number of unemployed people in the UK is measured through the Labour Force Survey following the internationally agreed definition recommended by the ILO (International Labour Organisation) – an agency of the United Nations.

Unemployed people:
- are without a job, want a job, have actively sought work in the last four weeks and are available to start work in the next two weeks, or
- are out of work, have found a job and are waiting to start it in the next two weeks

Other key indicators

Claimant count

The number of people claiming Jobseeker's Allowance benefits.

Earnings

A measure of the money people receive in return for work done, gross of tax. It includes salaries and, unless otherwise stated, bonuses but not unearned income, benefits in kind or arrears of pay.

Productivity

Whole economy output per worker is the ratio of Gross Value Added (GVA) at basic prices and Labour Force Survey (LFS) total employment. Manufacturing output per filled job is the ratio of manufacturing output (from the Index of Production) and productivity jobs for manufacturing (constrained to LFS jobs at the whole economy level).

Redundancies

The number of people who:

- were not in employment during the reference week, and
- reported that they had been made redundant in the month of, or the two calendar months prior to, the reference week

plus the number of people who:

- were in employment during the reference week, and
- started their job in the same calendar month as, or the two calendar months prior to, the reference week, and
- reported that they had been made redundant in the month of, or the two calendar months prior to, the reference week

Unit wage costs

A measure of the cost of wages and salaries per unit of output.

Vacancies

The statistics are based on ONS's Vacancy Survey of businesses. The survey is designed to provide comprehensive estimates of the stock of vacancies across the economy, excluding those in agriculture, forestry and fishing. Vacancies are defined as positions for which employers are actively seeking recruits from outside their business or organisation. More information on labour market concepts, sources and methods is available in the *Guide to Labour Market Statistics* at www.statistics.gov.uk/about/data/guides/LabourMarket/default.asp

Directory of online tables

The tables listed below are available as Excel spreadsheets via weblinks accessible from the main *Economic & Labour Market Review* (ELMR) page of the National Statistics website. Tables in sections 1, 3, 4 and 5 replace equivalent ones formerly published in *Economic Trends*, although there are one or two new tables here; others have been expanded to include, as appropriate, both unadjusted/seasonally adjusted, and current price/chained volume measure variants. Tables in sections 2 and 6 were formerly in *Labour Market Trends*. The opportunity has also been taken to extend the range of dates shown in many cases, as the online tables are not constrained by page size.

In the online tables, the four-character identification codes at the top of each data column correspond to the ONS reference for that series on our time series database. The latest data sets for the old *Economic Trends* tables and the Labour Market Statistics First Release tables are still available on this database via the 'Time Series Data' link on the National Statistics main web page. These data sets can also be accessed from links at the bottom of each section's table listings via the 'Data tables' link in the individual ELMR edition pages on the website.

Weblink: www.statistics.gov.uk/elmr/11_08/data_page.asp

Title	Frequency of update	Updated since last month
UK economic accounts		
1.01 National accounts aggregates	M	✔
1.02 Gross domestic product and gross national income	M	✔
1.03 Gross domestic product, by category of expenditure	M	✔
1.04 Gross domestic product, by category of income	M	•
1.05 Gross domestic product and shares of income and expenditure	M	•
1.06 Income, product and spending per head	Q	•
1.07 Households' disposable income and consumption	M	•
1.08 Household final consumption expenditure	M	•
1.09 Gross fixed capital formation	M	•
1.10 Gross value added, by category of output	M	✔
1.11 Gross value added, by category of output: service industries	M	✔
1.12 Summary capital accounts and net lending/net borrowing	Q	•
1.13 Private non-financial corporations: allocation of primary income account	Q	•
1.14 Private non-financial corporations: secondary distribution of income account and capital account	Q	•
1.15 Balance of payments: current account	M	✔
1.16 Trade in goods (on a balance of payments basis)	M	✔
1.17 Measures of variability of selected economic series	Q	•
1.18 Index of services	M	✔
Selected labour market statistics		
2.01 Summary of Labour Force Survey data	M	✔
2.02 Employment by age	M	✔
2.03 Full-time, part-time and temporary workers	M	✔
2.04 Public and private sector employment	Q	•
2.05 Workforce jobs	Q	•
2.06 Workforce jobs by industry	Q	✔
2.07 Actual weekly hours of work	M	✔
2.08 Usual weekly hours of work	M	✔
2.09 Unemployment by age and duration	M	✔
2.10 Claimant count levels and rates	M	✔
2.11 Claimant count by age and duration	M	✔
2.12 Economic activity by age	M	✔
2.13 Economic inactivity by age	M	✔
2.14 Economic inactivity: reasons	M	✔
2.15 Educational status, economic activity and inactivity of young people	M	✔
2.16 Average earnings – including bonuses	M	✔
2.17 Average earnings – excluding bonuses	M	✔
2.18 Productivity and unit wage costs	M	✔
2.19 Regional labour market summary	M	✔

Weblink: www.statistics.gov.uk/elmr/11_08/data_page.asp

2.20	International comparisons	M	✔
2.21	Labour disputes	M	✔
2.22	Vacancies	M	✔
2.23	Vacancies by industry	M	✔
2.24	Redundancies: levels and rates	M	✔
2.25	Redundancies: by industry	Q	•
2.26	Sampling variability for headline labour market statistics	M	✔

Prices

3.01	Producer and consumer prices	M	✔
3.02	Harmonised Indices of Consumer Prices: EU comparisons	M	✔

Selected output and demand indicators

4.01	Output of the production industries	M	✔
4.02	Engineering and construction: output and orders	M	✔
4.03	Motor vehicle and steel production	M	✔
4.04	Indicators of fixed investment in dwellings	M	✔
4.05	Number of property transactions	M	✔
4.06	Change in inventories	Q	•
4.08	Retail sales, new registrations of cars and credit business	M	✔
4.09	Inland energy consumption: primary fuel input basis	M	•

Selected financial statistics

5.01	Sterling exchange rates and UK reserves	M	✔
5.02	Monetary aggregates	M	✔
5.03	Counterparts to changes in money stock M4	M	✔
5.04	Public sector receipts and expenditure	Q	•
5.05	Public sector key fiscal indicators	M	✔
5.06	Consumer credit and other household sector borrowing	M	✔
5.07	Analysis of bank lending to UK residents	M	•
5.08	Interest rates and yields	M	✔
5.09	A selection of asset prices	M	✔

Further labour market statistics

6.01	Working-age households	A	•
6.02	Local labour market indicators by unitary and local authority	Q	•
6.03	Employment by occupation	Q	•
6.04	Employee jobs by industry	M	✔
6.05	Employee jobs by industry division, class or group	Q	✔
6.06	Employee jobs by region and industry	Q	✔
6.07	Key productivity measures by industry	M	✔
6.08	Total workforce hours worked per week	Q	✔
6.09	Total workforce hours worked per week by region and industry group	Q	✔
6.10	Job-related training received by employees	Q	•
6.11	Unemployment rates by previous occupation	Q	•
6.12	Average Earnings Index by industry: excluding and including bonuses	M	✔

Weblink: www.statistics.gov.uk/elmr/11_08/data_page.asp

6.13	Average Earnings Index: effect of bonus payments by main industrial sector	M	✔
6.14	Median earnings and hours by main industrial sector	A	•
6.15	Median earnings and hours by industry section	A	•
6.16	Index of wages per head: international comparisons	M	✔
6.17	Regional Jobseeker's Allowance claimant count rates	M	✔
6.18	Claimant count area statistics: counties, unitary and local authorities	M	✔
6.19	Claimant count area statistics: UK parliamentary constituencies	M	✔
6.20	Claimant count area statistics: constituencies of the Scottish Parliament	M	✔
6.21	Jobseeker's Allowance claimant count flows	M	✔
6.22	Number of previous Jobseeker's Allowance claims	Q	✔
6.23	Interval between Jobseeker's Allowance claims	Q	•
6.24	Average duration of Jobseeker's Allowance claims by age	Q	•
6.25	Vacancies by size of enterprise	M	•
6.26	Redundancies: re-employment rates	Q	•
6.27	Redundancies by Government Office Region	Q	•
6.28	Redundancy rates by industry	Q	•
6.29	Labour disputes: summary	M	✔
6.30	Labour disputes: stoppages in progress	M	✔

Notes

A Annually
Q Quarterly
M Monthly

More information

Time series are available from www.statistics.gov.uk/statbase/tsdintro.asp
Subnational labour market data are available from www.statistics.gov.uk/statbase/Product.asp?vlnk=14160 and www.nomisweb.co.uk
Labour Force Survey tables are available from www.statistics.gov.uk/statbase/Product.asp?vlnk=14365
Annual Survey of Hours and Earnings data are available from www.statistics.gov.uk/StatBase/Product.asp?vlnk=13101

Contact points

Recorded announcement of latest RPI
☎ 01633 456961
✉ rpi@ons.gsi.gov.uk

Labour Market Statistics Helpline
☎ 01633 456901
✉ labour.market@ons.gsi.gov.uk

Earnings Customer Helpline
☎ 01633 819024
✉ earnings@ons.gsi.gov.uk

National Statistics Customer Contact Centre
☎ 0845 601 3034
✉ info@statistics.gsi.gov.uk

Skills and Education Network
☎ 024 7682 3439
✉ senet@lsc.gov.uk

Department for Children, Schools and Families Public Enquiry Unit
☎ 0870 000 2288

For statistical information on

Average Earnings Index (monthly)
☎ 01633 819024

Claimant count
☎ 01633 456901

Consumer Prices Index
☎ 01633 456900
✉ cpi@ons.gsi.gov.uk

Earnings
Annual Survey of Hours and Earnings
☎ 01633 456120

Basic wage rates and hours for manual workers with a collective agreement
☎ 01633 819008

Low-paid workers
☎ 01633 819024
✉ lowpay@ons.gsi.gov.uk

Labour Force Survey
☎ 01633 456901
✉ labour.market@ons.gsi.gov.uk

Economic activity and inactivity
☎ 01633 456901

Employment
Labour Force Survey
☎ 01633 456901
✉ labour.market@ons.gsi.gov.uk

Employee jobs by industry
☎ 01633 456776

Total workforce hours worked per week
☎ 01633 456720
✉ productivity@ons.gsi.gov.uk

Workforce jobs series – short-term estimates
☎ 01633 456776
✉ workforce.jobs@ons.gsi.gov.uk

Labour costs
☎ 01633 819024

Labour disputes
☎ 01633 456721

Labour Force Survey
☎ 01633 456901
✉ labour.market@ons.gsi.gov.uk

Labour Force Survey Data Service
☎ 01633 455732
✉ lfs.dataservice@ons.gsi.gov.uk

New Deal
☎ 0114 209 8228

Productivity and unit wage costs
☎ 01633 456720

Public sector employment
General enquiries
☎ 01633 455889

Source and methodology enquiries
☎ 01633 812865

Qualifications (Department for Children, Schools and Families)
☎ 0870 000 2288

Redundancy statistics
☎ 01633 456901

Retail Prices Index
☎ 01633 456900
✉ rpi@ons.gsi.gov.uk

Skills (Department for Innovation, Universities & Skills)
☎ 0870 001 0336

Skill needs surveys and research into skill shortages
☎ 0870 001 0336

Small firms (BERR)
Enterprise Directorate
☎ 0114 279 4439

Subregional estimates
☎ 01633 812038

Annual employment statistics
✉ annual.employment.figures@ons.gsi.gov.uk

Annual Population Survey, local area statistics
☎ 01633 455070

Trade unions (BERR)
Employment relations
☎ 020 7215 5934

Training
Adult learning – work-based training (DWP)
☎ 0114 209 8236

Employer-provided training (Department for Innovation, Universities & Skills)
☎ 0870 001 0336

Travel-to-Work Areas
Composition and review
☎ 01329 813054

Unemployment
☎ 01633 456901

Vacancies
Vacancy Survey: total stocks of vacancies
☎ 01633 455070

ONS economic and labour market publications

ANNUAL

Financial Statistics Explanatory Handbook

2008 edition. Palgrave Macmillan, ISBN 0-230-52583-2. Price £47.50.

www.statistics.gov.uk/products/p4861.asp

Foreign Direct Investment (MA4)

2006 edition

www.statistics.gov.uk/products/p9614.asp

Input-Output analyses for the United Kingdom

2006 edition

www.statistics.gov.uk/products/p7640.asp

Research and development in UK businesses (MA14)

2006 edition

www.statistics.gov.uk/statbase/product.asp?vlnk=165

Share Ownership

2006 edition

www.statistics.gov.uk/products/p930.asp

United Kingdom Balance of Payments (Pink Book)

2007 edition. Palgrave Macmillan, ISBN 978-1-4039-9397-7. Price £49.50.

www.statistics.gov.uk/products/p1140.asp

United Kingdom National Accounts (Blue Book)

2007 edition. Palgrave Macmillan, ISBN 978-1-4039-9398-4. Price £49.50.

www.statistics.gov.uk/products/p1143.asp

First releases

- Annual survey of hours and earnings
- Foreign direct investment
- Gross domestic expenditure on research and development
- Low pay estimates
- Regional gross value added
- Share ownership
- UK Business enterprise research and development
- Work and worklessness among households

QUARTERLY

Consumer Trends

2008 quarter 1

www.statistics.gov.uk/products/p242.asp

United Kingdom Economic Accounts

2008 quarter 1. Palgrave Macmillan, ISBN 978-0-230-21759-1. Price £35.

www.statistics.gov.uk/products/p1904.asp

UK trade in goods analysed in terms of industry (MQ10)

2008 quarter 1

www.statistics.gov.uk/products/p731.asp

First releases

- Balance of payments
- Business investment
- GDP preliminary estimate
- Government deficit and debt under the Maastricht Treaty (six-monthly)
- International comparisons of productivity (six-monthly)
- Internet connectivity
- Investment by insurance companies, pension funds and trusts
- Productivity
- Profitability of UK companies
- Public sector employment
- Quarterly National Accounts
- UK output, income and expenditure

MONTHLY

Financial Statistics

July 2008. Palgrave Macmillan, ISBN 978-0-230-21741-6. Price £47.50.

www.statistics.gov.uk/products/p376.asp

Focus on Consumer Price Indices

June 2008

www.statistics.gov.uk/products/p867.asp

Monthly review of external trade statistics (MM24)

May 2008

www.statistics.gov.uk/products/p613.asp

Producer Price Indices (MM22)

June 2008

www.statistics.gov.uk/products/p2208.asp

First releases

- Consumer price Indices
- Index of production
- Index of services
- Labour market statistics
- Labour market statistics: regional
- Producer prices
- Public sector finances
- Retail sales
- UK trade

OTHER

The ONS Productivity Handbook: a statistical overview and guide

Palgrave Macmillan, ISBN 978-0-230-57301-7. Price £55.

www.statistics.gov.uk/about/data/guides/productivity/default.asp

Labour Market Review

2006 edition. Palgrave Macmillan, ISBN 1-4039-9735-7. Price £40.

www.statistics.gov.uk/products/p4315.asp

National Accounts Concepts, Sources and Methods

www.statistics.gov.uk/products/p1144.asp

Sector classification guide (MA23)

www.statistics.gov.uk/products/p7163.asp

Recent articles

Future articles

List is provisional and subject to change/reduction.